SOCIETY
and the SACRED

TOWARD A THEOLOGY OF
CULTURE IN DECLINE

LANGDON GILKEY

CROSSROAD · NEW YORK

1981
The Crossroad Publishing Company
575 Lexington Avenue, New York, NY 10022

Library of Congress Cataloging in Publication Data

Gilkey, Langdon Brown, 1919–
    Society and the sacred.

    1. Religion and culture—Addresses, essays, lectures.
I. Title.
BL65.C8G54   261   81-9775
ISBN 0-8245-0089-X   AACR2

For
Wilhelm Hermann Weber
of
Aalsmeer

CONTENTS

PREFACE

This volume is composed of a series of addresses and papers written over the past half decade or so and delivered, almost without exception, to college and university audiences. As a consequence of that "public"—as opposed, say, to a seminary or church audience—quite naturally these writings deal with the commonly shared issues of contemporary culture, society, and history rather than with intra-ecclesiastical or theological issues. These have been the issues which more than any others have puzzled, disturbed, and challenged my own thought in the recent past. As a result, these writings represent an example of a theology of culture rather than an example of systematic or constructive theology.

This rubric—theology of culture—is, I think, in this case thoroughly apt. This is not reflection directed at the phenomena of religion or of religious language, and asking questions about the character of the former and its relation to other concerns, and about the latter's meaning, validity, and relation to the languages of other disciplines. Such an enterprise is correctly called philosophy of religion. Rather here religious reflection is looking at society and seeking to understand the latter, much as economic, sociological, or political theorists might do, and with the same shared "object." And just as it is difficult for any one of them to analyze society without presupposing and using a particular interpretation of human community, without some fundamental social theory or other, so it is hard to view society from the standpoint of religious reflection without representing in one's thought a particular viewpoint *in* religion, that is, a particular stance vis-à-vis religion, its relation to human being, and its implications for reality as a whole. This is thus a *theology* of culture, an analysis of culture from a particular vantage point within religious reflection as a whole.

This is also a theology of culture because, in seeking to understand what is happening in contemporary culture and in the sequences of events that make up contemporary history, it asks questions about the *religious* dilemmas of cultural life and so questions guided by *theological* problems and concerns. By such religious or theological questions I mean questions of meaning or of meaninglessness, of the ambiguity even of creativity, of the freedom *and* the bondage of the will, of the strange, inexorable inheritance of evil, of the career of good and evil in the passage of time, of the contradiction of even our highest values, of the tension between affirmation and tolerance, between pluralism and truth, and of the promise of new possibilities and the need for hope for the future. These are questions implicitly raised and answered in all social theory and skirted in philosophy of religion. Such issues—as these writings show—are dealt with directly in theology of culture. Instead of exploring these issues in themselves or in relation to a particular religious community's symbols—as a given systematic theology might do—these questions are in the following studies found to appear naturally within the matrix of the culture's social and historical life. If this is so—and this is one of my main arguments—then an analysis of culture in terms of these questions, and thus in terms of the categories appropriate to these questions, is necessary if the contours of present cultural life and the ups and downs of its historical career are to be understood.

Two aspects of contemporary culture manifest themselves throughout these studies and can be said to form the constructive conclusions—or, if you will, the guiding presuppositions—of these thoughts. The first is that there is what can be called a "religious dimension" to cultural life making such an analysis imperative if certain undeniable aspects of culture are to be uncovered and understood. In the case of each subject taken up—contemporary science, technology, nationalism, ideologies, cultural pluralism—the religious dimension of that facet of culture is uncovered and the resultant religious dilemmas are described. If these analyses of culture make sense, that is, if a theological analysis seems to be dealing with real aspects and real problems of our public life, then this seems to vindicate the hypothesis that society in fact does possess a "sacred" dimension, a dimension to be analyzed in its own religious terms as well as by means of the other methods lodged in the biological and social sciences.

Secondly, most of the studies reflect another theme: the possible decline of the culture of the West. Clearly there can be no certainty here, for future history is both contingent and inscrutable (or inscrutable *because* it is contingent). Nevertheless these essays delineate certain fundamental trends that seem to point in that direction. An autumnal chill is in the air; its similarity to the chill in other periods of cultural decline is undeniable. One can point not only to vast shifts in geopolitical balances of power and influence but also to the apparent disintegration of our reigning contemporary ideologies (East and West alike). It is even more the sense—as the studies on science especially indicate—that the intellectual and spiritual heart of the culture, its confidence in science, technology and an expanding industrialism, has come upon difficult if not self-contradictory and self-destructive days, and that the culture as a whole is thus entering a "time of troubles" of very deep scope. As a consequence both social reflection in general and religious reflection in particular face quite new sorts of problems and challenges. It is this theme and its significance that the subtitle underlines: "Toward a Theology of Culture in Decline." This is not to say that our cultural values (our *true* values: freedom, rights, justice, and equality) will inexorably disappear in whatever new cultural synthesis may follow the present one. It is, however, certainly to warn that they will be genuinely endangered if, in order to preserve our own power, wealth, and security in a difficult and precarious time, we enact policies of international alliance and of national action that ignore, submerge, and thus sacrifice those same values. To gain briefly our life we may well lose our cultural integrity and any hope of the future continuance of that for which it stands.

This volume is affectionately dedicated to my father-in-law Wim (Opi) Weber of Aalsmeer, the Netherlands. Although, needless to say, I have had him primarily in view when I chose this dedication, nevertheless possibly the "aura" of the gratitude and affection represented there can also radiate beyond his person to my entire adopted family in the Netherlands, and even to all those friends there—and in Köln—who have so vastly enriched my life since the time, some years ago, when as a son-in-law I became one of them. However, it is primarily "Opi" whom I have in mind: elegant and thoughtful father-in-law, superb and beloved grandfather ("Opi"), skillful and indefatigable sailor, he has in these last years meant more to all of us than can easily be put into words.

Finally I want also to thank especially Martha Morrow for her friendship and in this case for her help in preparing these essays for publication. And to my love, Sonja, and to Frouwkje, Amos, and Whitney I am as always more than grateful. Quite literally there is little of worth and excitement in life without love and those whom we can love—and they provide more of both than this author deserves.

Langdon Gilkey

The Divinity School
The University of Chicago

The SACRED
and MODERN
CULTURE

1

THE NEW WATERSHED
IN THEOLOGY

It seems to many contemporary observers that in the latter half of the
twentieth century we find ourselves in the midst of cognitive, cultural, and sociopolitical changes of vast importance, possibly of the
scope represented by the development of Enlightenment sensibilities in
the seventeenth and eighteenth centuries. That these changes are in fact
of that depth and scope is by no means certain; it is impossible even in
the midst of the most important historical transformations clearly to see
what is afoot. Only afterwards can historical commentators see that a
new epoch has begun or an old one ended. Let us settle for the fact that
it *feels* as if we were reaching the end of a historical era, and that reflection on the elements that make up that feeling tends to substantiate it.
If this be so, then this is important in turn for theological reflection.
Since the Enlightenment, theology has found itself, almost whether it
will or no, proceeding with its work in the closest relation to the developing culture of modernity. Although much theology sought to ignore
or deny that relation, still the relation was effectively there whether as
one of welcoming acceptance and accommodation or one of enthusiastic,
if ultimately unsuccessful, antagonism. It was much as in patristic theology, which both accepted and yet also in part attempted to reject
Hellenistic culture. In both the latter cases, the main or predominant
effort of patristic theology was to interpret the gospel in terms of the
culture, to give Christianity a Hellenistic form and/or Hellenistic culture a Christian form.

Now if these intimations of vast cultural change are accurate, and if

3

we are in fact witnessing the beginning of the decline of the Enlightenment, then clearly theology must reflect on the implications of that possibility both for theological method and theological content, in fact, it must seek to relate itself in distinctly new ways to its changing cultural world. What these new ways ought to be is by no means yet clear, for the shape of the new cultural whole, if there is to be one, remains quite hidden. Nevertheless, it may well be both possible and expedient to survey the cultural situation around us with the possibility in mind that an era might be closing, in order to explore the implications for theology of these developments. And in any case, such fundamental cultural shifts, merely in their occurrence, inexorably raise new and important theological problems as they proceed on their course, problems that tend to move quickly center stage. It is, then, both in order to understand the new, possibly disintegrating, shape of our cultural situation—of the "modernity" in which we were all raised up—and in order to reflect on the theological problems raised thereby that we embark on what we have called the diagnosis of the new watershed confronting Christian theology.

The shifts we are talking about can, we agree, be roughly grouped under four headings. Each in its own way represents to us "an ending of the Enlightenment," a terminal symptom of some fundamental aspect of the culture that has formed our contemporary world.

1. The Enlightenment saw itself as representing a new era for human history on three major grounds: (a) Correct, cumulative, and fruitful methods of knowing had been discovered and developed; with science "we now know how to know," and through that expanding knowledge we can count on an increasing control over the various natural forces threatening human welfare. (b) The practical application of this new and expanding knowledge of "causes" in an expanding technology and through that in an expanding industrialism would provide the unquestioned blessing of a plethora of goods for general consumption. With the banishing of ignorance, poverty could also be banished. (c) The curse of traditional superstition and of unexamined authority (especially in religion) could now be itself eradicated, making rational, political, legal, social, and moral structures possible for the first time in history.

Our century has seen each of these grounds for optimism radically questioned, if not shattered—or, like Hegel's absolute at the hands of Marx, each "turned on its head." What was promised has either not in fact occurred, or, if it has occurred, new problems, even contradictions, even lethal dilemmas, have resulted. In any case, if (and the case is a good one) the Enlightenment epoch can be defined as centered about these three convictions or "dreams," that epoch could now be said to be ending with the radical falsification each one of these has undergone in our own lifetime.

The counterfactual data to these hopes are multiple. (a) Although throughout the career of this culture movements have appeared that have questioned the omnicompetence of science, that raised objections to its claim to be the sole avenue to cognitive touch with reality (e.g., Romanticism, Neo-Kantianism, Whiteheadianism, Existentialism, etc.), still the sense of the ambiguity of the scientific consciousness has today grown to large proportions—and now worries even the National Science Foundation's public relations division. Scientific medicine has long been taken as *the* paradigm of Enlightenment science and its obvious benefits; at present, no profession finds itself so sharply criticized for its ignorance regarding health matters as well as for its greed (something like the clergy in the late medieval period!). (b) Technology has produced means of destruction that more than balance its beneficent creations—and there seems no human (rational) way to stop these "historical" developments. (c) The plethora of goods has arrived on schedule. It has, however, caused the ever-widening disparity of their distribution to engender deep and increasing enmities and recurrent conflicts; and it has signally failed to pursue, much less capture, "happiness" even in those who have the goods. (d) Most important, we are suddenly aware that technical industrialism—in expanding as the Enlightenment hoped—threatens to destroy the nature system and to use up the natural resources on which we all depend—another "historical" process that it seems impossible either to stop or to control.

Like the characters in "The Monkey's Paw," modern culture has gotten precisely what it thought it wanted, but then has found it when it arrived utterly menacing. It has developed autonomy only to find it sliding into an infinitely relative and narcissistic subjectivity. It has sought successfully to subjugate and dominate ("objectify") nature for its own purposes, and then, finding these purposes largely ignoble (concupiscent), menaced itself through that very domination (even while it said officially that we are "only a part of nature"). It sought to be "rational" and thus to exclude all that could not be proved, in fact, anything that could not be empirically nailed down; as a consequence it has found cross-disciplinary speech impossible, and consideration of, much less reverence for, standards, fundamental aims, or important purposes onerous. It has sought to rationalize social existence and created problems for strong individuals and for community alike. It sought to eradicate the religious, only to find in our century demonic social faiths (ideologies) dominating its historical scene, new and exotic religious cults (even the occult) replacing our tamed churches, and an upsurge of radical fundamentalist religion hitched to, rather than eradicated by, the technological culture. In each case, the human intellectual creativity represented by the Enlightenment has revealed itself not only as ambiguous but also as potentially lethal in its consequences. The dilemma of the culture is apparently essential because it is precisely its creativity and its success in enacting its most cherished forms, not its failure to enact these forms, that threatens its life—thus does it seem difficult to see how *it* could generate an answer.

2. The second aspect of the new watershed concerns dramatic and perhaps crucial shifts in the power and in the influence of the Enlightenment culture. Certainly part of the grounds for the confidence in itself that characterized the Enlightenment culture was the fact that politically, militarily, and economically it could not be—and was not—challenged by any external cultural force. Quite possibly as a consequence, its intellectual, political, moral, and religious "superstructure" became also dominant, that is, was considered clearly superior, not only by its happy protagonists but also (and here is the key point) by the unhappy inhabitants of other cultures seeking fruitlessly (at first) to resist its cultural power, as, for example, in nineteenth-century China. This domination up and down the line (from "gun boats to crosses," from industrial technology and economic organization to autonomous [based on personal choice] marriage, and so on up to political democracy, humanitarianism, and religion) is no longer the case on *any* level. From 1456 (when the Turks last challenged Vienna) to 1940—five hundred years!— no non-Western power could threaten a major European power, and certainly not all of the latter together (no wonder they thought history was progress!). Now *no* European power is a major power, and only one of the present four is "Western" in inheritance, that is, a culture formed by the Enlightenment—a dramatic collapse of relative power that will be increasingly evident in subsequent historical events.

Correspondingly, the social ideals generated out of the Enlighten-

ment—individual rights, political freedom, democratic processes, etc.—
no longer "grasp" persons in other cultural and social situations as ideals
for them—as they did at the end of the eighteenth and throughout the
nineteenth centuries. Rather, they appear as "suspect," as ideologies that
are covers for special privileges and for selfish materialism—an assessment that is hard to argue with. The science, the technology and the
industrialism of the West have spread—and create their own nemesis.
The ideals, the personal and social symbols that animated Enlightenment creativity, seem to be moribund, languishing in a global Suburban
Captivity (even deeper than that of the ecclesia), mouthed by every dic-
tator—and, ironically (hopefully?), real only among the almost hopeless
dissidents in Eastern Europe, in Russia, and in China. As the scientific
consciousness, technology, and industrialism of the Enlightenment have
encountered *their* problems in our time, so the economic, political, and
military power of Western culture and the force of its ideational or symbolic structure seem also to be encountering massive problems. To become the ideological justification of remaining islands of feudal privilege
and totalitarian tyranny is almost as ironic a fate for the social ideals of
the French philosophes as was that suffered by the message of the Cross
as an ideology for the ancien régime!

3. The third point possibly indicative of a severe fissure in modern
post-Enlightenment culture has been termed the "collapse of salvation
history." One might sum up our remarks to date as follows: the scientific consciousness represented the cognitive heart of Enlightenment culture, scientific technology the ground of its deepest and most concrete
hopes, and the economic, political, and military power of the West the
foundation for its sense of continuing security, reality, and power. With
the beginnings, or apparent beginnings, of the disintegration of these
three bases for its self-confidence, therefore, one may well expect that
the predominant, guiding, and empowering ethos or myth of the culture—the dramatic "story" expressive of its global conquest, domination, and glory—would also begin to collapse. That is, if Western culture has believed anything about itself in history, if it has affirmed a
historical destiny or vocation for itself (and it did), it has expressed this
"religious substance" in its own form of a "salvation history," a story of
the victory of good over evil in unfolding time in which it bore a crucial, in fact *the* crucial, role. To consideration of this deepest level of the
potential collapse—and watershed—we now turn.

Not every culture, of course, expresses its "religious substance," its fundamental mythos or story about itself, as a salvation *history*, that is, as a story which establishes the meaning of the culture, its grounds for security and confidence, its ultimate legitimacy, power, glory, and destiny in terms of a story concerned with the historical process. There are other possibilities for this security, legitimacy, power, and glory: perhaps parentage and inauguration by divine beings, perhaps through being the mediator, steward, or representative of the divine, and so on. Here Western culture shows its Judeo-Christian heritage. For in that heritage, divine activity, presence, and the gift of salvation have appeared in and through a special sequence of historical events and thus form a salvation history: in the Jewish version, history is centered on the covenant people and moves forward under the divine providence to the messianic reign to come; in the Christian instance, where history is centered on the Christ and the church and moves forward (in a variety of interpretations) under providence to the Kingdom.

A good case could be made that the spiritual substance of the Enlightenment took its shape *against* the Hebraic and the then predominant Christian myths or salvation histories. In the case of Christianity, this was the story of the divine participation in and guidance of a fallen historical process now being illumined, ordered, redeemed, and renewed through Christ, his church, and "Christendom," a "myth" witnessed to in Scripture and formulated by both Catholic and Protestant traditional theologies. In its place, the Enlightenment set its *own* salvation history, its own understanding of the revelatory and redemptive character of historical process. This was the "theory of progress," spawned by (as its "Protestant principle") an initial and risky rational skepticism about and criticism of traditions, and sustained by (as its "Catholic substance") an accumulating learning, made up of scientific knowledge, technical know-how, more and more practical and open social laws and customs, and ever-advancing moral and social ideals. Whereas the Christian salvation history was now regarded as prescientific myth and incredible, a function of human immaturity, ignorance, and weakness, this one, as the product of science, was simply regarded as true. After all, science, technology, and their benevolent consequences certainly seemed to be accumulating on every side, and Western modes of existing and of ideals were spreading in a dramatic fashion across the globe: progress could thus simply be *induced* from the evident facts of history. With the appearance of the nineteenth-century concept of evolution, this induction from common experience could now claim to be "science," that is, to be not only an empirical given but also able to be exhibited as both a basis for and an implication of the most fundamental and inclusive theory, namely, that of a general theory of evolution or development. Thus, as always, did the content and the epistemology of the mythical center of a culture's religious substance come finally into accord with one another. Theological conceptions of the meaning of history—unless they adopted this Enlightenment schema and themselves became liberal progressivist—made almost no headway against this predominant mythos: epistemologically and ontologically, the Christian mythos seemed to deny the empirical and naturalistic canons of the Enlightenment, and in ethos the Christian story of fall and redemption seemed neurotic, if not perverse and self-serving, to generations who saw all of history quite obviously (read "empirically") as a gradual development from early chaos to their own resplendent order.

Meanwhile, another form of Western salvation history had appeared, developed in radical opposition to and criticism of its older Enlightenment sibling. This was, of course, the Marxist-Leninist salvation history, accepting from the previous Judeo-Christian religious heritage the sense of history as an unfolding meaning leading to a culmination, and from the Enlightenment the confidence in science, technology, and industrialism. It challenged, however, because of their ambiguity for the proletariat of maturing industrial societies (evident by the mid-nineteenth century), the Enlightenment confidence in a preestablished harmony of prudent self-concern, the creative workings of the free market and of the democratic process, and the sanctity of private property. Characteristically, it was even more impatient with the Jewish and Christian salvation histories than had been the bourgeois scientific and naturalistic viewpoint which replaced them.

There were, then, two different versions of salvation history which provided the spiritual substance for post-Englightenment scientific, technical, and industrial culture. Whereas the liberal-bourgeois version has in the twentieth century suffered loss both of economic, political, and military dominance and of its "grasping power" as an ideology, the Marxist one has gained in the mode of political and military dominance (and now rules at least half of the "have" world), lost in its grasping power wherever that power has spread and now rules, and has remained roughly steady (though of this I am by no means sure) as a major ideological force in the Third World.

These shifts in power we have already mentioned; let us, therefore, concentrate on the fate of the two schemes of salvation history, on the present status of the two ideologies spawned out of the Enlightenment. Both are, it seems to me, seriously, if not mortally, wounded. For both these schemes of historical meaning were originally regarded as "science"; each was the product of the confident and speculative period of expanding science when global concepts and systems came easily and appeared as simply verifiable and so as themselves merely "science." As historical counterfactual materials (anomalies) to both have mounted, their claim to be science has lost much of its credibility to all but the deeply faithful. They have appeared as "convictions," "beliefs," "doctrines," "truths" important for science, for Western culture, for sanity, etc.; thus, of course, as objects of faith, they are now vulnerable to criticism. As a consequence, the empirical and skeptical side of the scientific consciousness has been gnawing steadily at them: few scientists now easily include under "evolutionary laws" laws governing the development of history, or find progress a hypothesis easy to establish or verify by any of their methods—though they may well believe and even assume both. And belief in the Material Dialectic as "science" seems now to be confined to official propagandists and spokesmen.

More important has been the evidence counterfactual to both visions of social progress, especially progress defined as eradicating the massive evils of history: injustice, oppression, violence, and war. Much of this we have rehearsed in our discussion of the ambiguity of science and the lethal dangers for the future implied in technological advance. Perhaps even more effective has been the deep experience of evil in present history that the twentieth century brought along with it. Progressive optimists had recognized the depth and reality of the evil in the past, and its lingering power well into our present. What they had not expected were new and more virulent forms of evil generated in our present "civilized" world and out of its own essential structures. World War I, fascism, World War II, the Holocaust, Stalinism have so functioned (cf. the common remark in the thirties, "How could *this* happen in the twentieth century?"). Subsequently, the liberal-democratic-capitalistic world has itself had to face a barrage of accusations from those disadvantaged by *them* that they too (and not just the evil Fascists) represent classic forms of historical evil: of arrogance, oppression, exploitation, and brutalization. To a civilization that had long regarded itself as the apogee of moral and social, as well as technological and organizational, progress, the accusation by blacks, by women, and by the Third World that this so-called universal civilization was in actuality an instrument of white, male, Northern Hemispheric dominance and exploitation was particularly unsettling. One notes that few of the conservative leaders (that is, social and political adherents of Adam Smith and of John Locke) now speak of the progress and expansion of their cherished world. It is rather a matter of "holding the line," of "retaining and preserving" their sacred values, of "defending our kind of world" against aggressors. The salvation history of progress seems to have distintegrated as *future progress* into a quest for historical survival, for ways of avoiding historical extinction. Implicit here is a quite different vision of history's career.

Interestingly, it is not so different in the Marxist-Leninist worlds. There, largely because of the counterfactual evidence of oppressive totalitarianism in socialist countries, the grasping power of the myth has dwindled. In fact, in Poland, Eastern Europe, China, and probably Russia, this myth now appears (as did Christian Orthodoxy in its declining day and as did capitalistic dogma in its declining day) as an ideological instrument of oppression, a scheme of empty ideals or symbols useful only for the retention of power by a ruling elite. That history is to be increasingly dominated by the kind of Communist government that now oppresses them, and that that domination has a *saving* character, these populations—insofar as they manifest any political "self-consciousness"—neither believe nor wish to believe. The three salvation histories characteristic of our epoch, therefore—one of them, the Christian, lingering on, weakened, and on the defensive; the other two once quite dominant in our developing cultural life—now seem alike to be in a terminal state, held to only by "believers," and apparently, wherever they rule, quite without the power to galvanize adherents and so to provide unity, direction, standards, and courage to their respective communities.

One important qualification: these two Enlightenment salvation histories do remain important and creative—and relatively genuine—among dissidents, and, interestingly, among the dissidents in the cultures ruled by their own opposite number. When one listens to dissident voices in the Communist world—to workers in Poland, intellectuals in Russia, writers of wall posters in China, sufferers from the totalitarian oppression of the socialist-Communist regimes—one hears again the authentic ideals, norms, and hopes of the French Enlightenment, of Jefferson and Jackson, of the Bill of Rights, and so of the democratic-liberal movement—and *its* salvation history comes alive. When one listens to genuine dissidents in Western Europe, in Central and South America, and in Africa, one can hear the revolutionary aims and ideals of "socialism" argued, believed, and persuasively affirmed. Much like the Christian salvation history (and Buddhist), these "secular" salvation histories have died only in the cultures where they have achieved dominant power. Quite possibly, therefore, they will not disappear if this Enlightenment world suffers *itself* a radical transformation, but rather—as has happened before—provide elements for the new ideological mix (as Jewry and Christendom did earlier) that will arise in some new world. Certainly some sort of synthesis, now hidden, of the eighteenth-century emphasis on individual political rights and the nineteenth-century emphasis on corporate economic responsibility is the deepest need of our social future. In any case, and that is my present point, our time is apparently witnessing the gradual disintegration of its reigning "salvation histories" or ideologies, a fact which, if true, has immense implications for theological reflection—as it does for that reappearance of the religious in a wide variety of nonhistorical and even nonmodern forms referred to above.

4. The final element of the watershed has no particularly tragic or menacing aura—but it *does* set new and important issues and problems for theology. Of a certainty, this element is itself a function or consequence of each of the points outlined above. This is the present close encounter of religions, representing an encounter of a quite new kind. What is new about this encounter is the equality among religions that characterizes it, equality, one might say, of truth and of grace, of illuminating and of healing power. Like individuals in Enlightenment social theory, each religion now appears as a substantial individual, characterized by inherent and equal powers, privileges, and rights; the former developmental hierarchy of religions, with Christianity at the top, has quite vanished. The religious/theological categories of other religions (karma, identity, "Divine Soul," the shakras, psychic communion, etc.) now appear to many as potent thematizations of reality, rather than as "primitive" or bizarre notions out of touch with reality; the meditative techniques of Zen, yoga, chanting, mantras, and so on for many represent once "lost" but now recovered techniques with real saving power rather than premodern ways of "abandoning reality." And the ethics of other religions seem to offer modes of authentic life fully rivaling, if not surpassing, our own. The encounter is now fully one of equals.

This is, I think, a function of the first three points here listed: the ambiguity of the modern scientific consciousness, the loss of Western political and spiritual dominance, the death of the Western deity of progress. The dominance of Christianity based on its dogmatic claims had already been roundly criticized by the Enlightenment itself and Christianity itself subsequently relativized; as a consequence, liberal Christianity interpreted itself in Enlightenment categories and viewed itself as the "culmination" of religions largely because the culture of which it was the religious expression was clearly the culmination of civilization. For most of the period from 1850 to 1950, Christian superiority, therefore, was as much a function of Western as of Christian dogmatic superiority or even of both together. It was as the religion of the civilized West, through the latter's historical and this-worldly consciousness, its humanitarian ideals, its democratic morality, its monogamous family, its autonomy, its high evaluation of the person and so on that Christianity appeared as "superior"—and not through its own earlier dogmatic claims (cf. Schleiermacher, Ritschl, Max Müller, Harnack, Troeltsch, Hocking, and a host of others). And against other religions, it argued on the basis of that cultural superiority, not on dogmatic grounds, for its own truth and validity as the supreme religion, the absolute religion, the culmination of religion. Thus, with the decline of its "superior" cultural base, and with the penetration of its own turf by these once moribund rivals, Christianity (and Judaism as well) has found itself in a quite new, vulnerable, and interesting situation, a situation fundamentally different from that of an early Christianity surrounded by paganism, of medieval or Reformation "Christendom," and from the nineteenth-century situation of the Enlightenment/Protestant synthesis, in all of which (though on different grounds) Christianity regarded itself, if not as the sole possessor of truth and grace, at the least as the supreme and so superior example of them.

This situation is, therefore, quite new. It represents a veritable uncharted sea for theology, where neither the menacing rocks nor the clear channels are known—or even if there be water on which to sail the theological craft! What this situation calls for theologically is by no means clear—though it is clear that it is beset with baffling problems and perhaps mortal issues. What happens when one recognizes, and not grudgingly but *willingly* so, the truth and grace, the spiritual power of another faith (for example, Buddhism)—which we all now have to do? How does such a recognition, necessary for one's own honesty as well as for dialogue, feed back on our own theological understanding of our faith? If it demolishes the latter—if we say ours has no truth and grace, nor even a "special" truth and grace—then we no longer represent any religious position at all, and the dialogue, and the theological problem itself, cease. We have either become Buddhist or secular. And (let us note) the problem of affirming a relative stance still remains even in *that* subsequent dialogue, now between our Buddhist friend and ourselves as only "secular" students of other religions. And surely we do not want our counterpart to resign his or her position, to cease being Buddhist, to cease affirming the supreme validity of "the higher consciousness," and so on. Thus it appears that we must adopt a strangely paradoxical stance, namely, that at one and the same time we affirm our own stance and faith, and yet also recognize theirs—a not impossible and quite creative *personal* attitude but a difficult if not contradictory *theoretical* one. For it raises all sorts of theological problems: how to recognize the frequently superior spiritual power in them and to understand that theologically; how, therefore, to understand "revelation" to include them as well as our own foundation; how to rethink the "decisiveness of Christ" so as to maintain the latter and yet to include them; how to understand the truth in their view, e.g., in their anthropology, and yet to affirm one's own; how to recognize the obvious superiority of their view of nature and yet to understand that recognition theologically; and, perhaps most difficult of all, how to discover God (?) through Zazen or yoga (which is not at all hard) and yet to understand that uncovering theologically.

This is, to me, an uncharted sea. The Scriptures are themselves of little *direct* help (or so it seems to me); there is no recognized tradition of responsible reflection to succor us; and the few brave would-be pilots in our own time who have sailed forth into the unknown (Panikkar, W. C. Smith, Schuon, Rahner, Huston Smith, etc.) are (again, in my view) more to be congratulated for their courage than for their felicitous results. Nevertheless, personal experience and the wider encounter of cultures and religions force from us and from the Christian community a responsible, relevant, and contemporary theological word, a quite new Word. We are in the difficult, though intriguing, position of having at one and the same time to speak an illuminating, healing and transcendent Word to our culture's increasing agony and yet, as a kind of continuation of the Enlightenment even after its own termination (and, as noted, *because* of it), to recognize with quite new seriousness the relativity of our faith which these encounters with other religions force upon us all.

2

THE PHILOSOPHY OF
RELIGION IN OUR TIME

The subject of the philosophy of religion is as broad as the universe and the human existence which each, philosophy and religion, seeks to understand and to explicate. Consequently, many quite different kinds of things are going on there, dependent on what the view of what philosophy is, of what religion is, and of what the big issues and interesting problems are in our present existence. One may say there are four general areas of discussion in the philosophy of religion: (1) the relation of religion to the methods and results of the special sciences: physical, social, psychological, and historical; (2) the relations of religious traditions to one another, of, say, Buddhism to Christianity; (3) the relation of religion and theology to philosophy itself, that is, to linguistic, logical, epistemological, and metaphysical issues; (4) the relation of religion to other areas of cultural life, to morals, politics, the arts—the theology of culture and of society. In these remarks, I am going to deal with issues in (1) and (4), the relation of religion to the methods and results of the special sciences and the relation of religion to culture.

To try to talk philosophically of the relation of other religious traditions to Christianity is of vast present significance, but it comprises a whole topic in itself which I will broach later in this book. The relation to philosophical and so to metaphysical issues usefully comes last and not first. This is partly because if one major modern problem for religion is the question whether there is any meaning and use to religious and theological language, precisely the same problem seems to have arisen for metaphysical language. What is *its* meaning and use: in life, in the

15

special disciplines and sciences, in culture? Strangely enough, there are
not many more people in a university or a college who would give you
a more positive or self-assured answer to that question than to the same
question addressed to religious language. A discussion between these
two, between metaphysics and theology, unless well-grounded first,
seems more like an argument between two patients in a terminal ward
than it is a contest between powerful voices claiming our attention.

In any case, out of this division into areas of actual discussion we can
at least get some idea of what philosophy of religion is. A preliminary
definition or description might be: it is the form of talk that arises
whenever religion and something else are talked about: religion and science, religion and philosophy, religion and other religions, religion and
society or culture—and as one might summarize this, religion and general experience. Note, this is true with other disciplines as well as with
religion. Whenever persons in any science, social science, or humanistic
discipline—for example, history—talk about the relation of their work
to other disciplines—for example, the relation of historical method to
the methods of the natural sciences—it is talking philosophy. Philosophy is the realm of discourse within which disparate realms of discourse
talk—or try to talk—to one another. It corresponds in the realm of the
mind to the faculty club, or the administration offices, in a college.
Clearly, it is utterly essential to the unity and coherence of cultural life;
it is the only earthly antidote to the Tower of Babel. Modern special
disciplines have systematically questioned the use or the meaning of
philosophical discourse: "We don't need it in our laboratories or depart-
mental meetings." Of course not, any more than they would need deans
there! Then these same special disciplines have looked at the university
as a whole, regretted its disunity, the inability of its disciplines to talk
to one another, to discuss common presuppositions, standards and ends,
and moaned that their world was divided into separate worlds!

Much can and has been said about the relation of the special sciences
to religion. For example, in our day much has been said about the relation of biology to religion in regard to the question of evolution, of
geology to religion in regard to the question of the age of the world, of
psychology to religion in regard to the question of religion as a projected
wish, a form of neurosis. And much in each case can be said in return
on the side of religion. I shall here concentrate on a more general problem raised for religion by the special sciences as a whole, a problem that

has, one may say, dominated the philosophy of religion for two or three decades.

Nothing has been more important for our life and our thinking than the rise of the natural sciences. It has, of course, transformed our powers to transform our environment; and so it has transformed both our world and our relation to it. But it has also changed many of our ideas, ideas about the universe, about its history, about our place in it, and so on, all very relevant to questions of religion. But of immediate interest to us, it has transformed our understanding of knowing, that is to say, of how to know. Or put differently, of how we relate to the truth: how to get it, if we can, and how to know we have gotten it once we have.

The development of this new understanding of truth cannot be traced here. In summary, it has meant that in relating to the truth, however much imagination may be there—and much is necessary—however much abstract relations of concepts, for example in mathematics, may be used—and much use of them is necessary—nevertheless, the source and ground of relevant truth, and its verification or falsification, lies for a scientific culture in experience, in sharable or common experience. Whatever authoritative people say or have said, whatever our guesses or intuitions may tell us, whatever sheer logic apparently may indicate, nothing is certain or even probable unless it is checked in experience, and nothing is really meaningful unless its source in the application to experience is made plain. The role of theory is to interpret, explain, and thus to transform and reshape experience. Unless it does this—and this is its test—it is impossible to know what that theory says or is even about.

This new view of truth slowly penetrated our culture as the role and authority of science increased. It had devastating results on traditional religion. It was devastating first of all because it questioned all unexamined authorities, whether of church or of Scripture, and secondly because what science discovered about the stars, about the age of the world, the origin and mechanics of life, the interrelations of species contradicted older "doctrines" on these same subjects and seemed to render much of the miraculous content of religion—now or in the past—simply incredible.

In various ways, religious thought has adjusted to this scientific impact. This process has been termed in general liberal religion, and most of those early problems were settled. But one has remained and has, as I noted, dominated the philosophy of religion. If all theories, ideas, or beliefs have meaning and validity—reference and credibility—solely insofar as they are locatable in definite, sharable experience, what meaning and validity do religious ideas under these conditions have? Can we point to the place in experience where God appears and where anyone who wishes to look can see him? If we cannot, how do we know he is there at all—except that others say he is; and how do we even know what the word might mean, what the concept is, if there is nowhere where we can point, if that concept thematizes or organizes no aspect of our common experience?

An older tradition would have answered these questions quickly enough. Look at the miracles of faith, they would say: in the Bible, in sacred history, in the experiences of being healed, reborn, or of prayer. As Billy Graham answered this question: I know God is there, I spoke to him last night. Here, in *these* experiences, God seems clearly to be at work. This is and remains a potent answer for many. But note how in this form it runs into other problems raised by a scientific culture: the problem of the appeal to authority and the problem of the credibility of miracle. Is a miracle credible or provable unless one already believes in God? asked David Hume. He answered, as most of us would, that a miracle is credible and assertable only if we *already* believe in God. If this be so, a miracle can't answer the question whether God is there at all.

A more satisfactory answer—at least so it seems to me—has two forms, a reflective and an experiential side. The reflective side—that is to say, the philosophy of religion answer—is: if special experiences don't help, then it is best to uncover and disclose those areas or aspects of general experience, of our ordinary experience of being and of doing whatever we do, and in those areas letting the religious dimensions of that experience manifest themselves to us. For if one holds theologically that God is the ever-present ground of all of our existence and all of our creative activity, then necessarily our being and our activity will in every facet disclose a religious dimension. And this can, possibly, be uncovered and so it will disclose itself to us as the referent of our religious speech, that which this speech is about, and so a crucial aspect of the meaning of that speech. To do this in part will be the aim of the rest of this study. The other answer, more experiential than reflective, has occurred widely through meditation. There, in Yoga, Zen, and Sufi matrices especially, the religious dimension of existence—however it may be named—has been widely *re*experienced in our time, without direct conflict with scientific or technological truth, and with vast healing power to our bodily selves and our inwardness. The results of this, widespread as it is—have not yet appeared prominently in our Western discussions of the philosophy of religion; but I suspect they will.

My second illustration of what the philosophy of religion is doing carries the question we have unearthed a little further, namely, the question what use or meaning does religious language have in ordinary experience, or, in a deeper form of that question, where does the sacred and the ultimate to which religious language refers—or seeks to refer or thinks it refers—appear in ordinary common experience? In this second illustration, we encounter two special sciences concerned with society, anthropology and sociology, each of which has uncovered a most interesting characteristic of social existence for a philosopher of religion, namely, the crucial role of the "religious," the sacred, and the ultimate in the life and even the very existence of social communities. Not that all anthropologists and sociologists agree that there is a crucial religious factor, if we may call it that, in social existence. Still, a surprising number of them do, whatever conclusions they may draw about the origins of this factor and its relation to what is ultimately "real." One thinks, of course, of Émile Durkheim and Auguste Comte, founders of sociology; of de Tocqueville, Simmel, and Weber; and in our own day of Parsons, Bellah, Berger, Luckmann, and Geertz—and in his own way, of the Marxist Ernst Bloch.

What these students of society have found—if I may give them a very hasty summary—is that any community or society is held together in sharing in, expressing and devoting themselves to, something sacred and ultimate—or a sacrality and an ultimacy—that permeates their life together, holds them together, directs their common life, and makes that common life possible. Thus, the common patterns of work and relation—the "meanings" of common life—have a shared value or worth that is by all who share in it regarded as ultimate, of supreme worth. The rules of behavior—the dos and the don'ts—that make social relations possible have an ultimate and sacral authority, and impose a sacred obligation. The shared symbols and myths that interpret the society's existence—its founding, its security in time, its destiny—that provide the basis for the society's self-interpretation and identity—and thus for all its standards for action and for goals—are also sacral in character. These roles, rules, and ultimate symbols *constitute* the society, that is, its substance and identity, are central to it in both its being and its particular character. Correspondingly, sharing in them by commitment and devotion constitutes a member of the society. Thus, this "substance," as Paul Tillich called it, is central to the society and to the relation of every member to it. As Durkheim said, society has for the individual in it a *religious* authority, power, and value, and hence it is and prospers. Or, as Tillich put it, every society has a religious substance which it shares and expresses in all aspects of its cultural life and in which we participate insofar as we are members.

This seems, of course, clear enough when we look at primitive societies with their tribal gods, their craft deities, their religious taboos, and their founding myths making legitimate and worthful each of their roles and duties. It is also clear when we look at premodern societies with their divinely established rulers, their divinely sanctioned moral codes, their established and crucial "churches," essential—so it was believed—to the society's life, security, and well-being. Here, as in primitive societies, religion permeates, authorizes, establishes, makes legitimate, and governs—spiritually if not externally—all aspects of the social life of men and women: their laws and courts, their customs and habits, their pleasures and vices, their most exalted and their lowliest roles—and even their Departments of Defense. Religion's myths answer the deepest questions about our identity, our origins, our destiny—and the meaning of life in time and so of our life—and that of our wider community in history. For this reason, because religion established, guaranteed, and preserved society's life, religions *were* established by their societies: that is, paid for and organized by the society, protected by it as essential to the society's life—much as modern science is essential to the workings of the present Defense Department. Thus did Marx say: criticism of religion is the beginning of all criticism. No social order can be challenged and refashioned unless its religious substance, the sacrality of its institutions, symbols, and myths, is itself first challenged. Ironically enough, this insight would now apply to present Communist Russia as it did then to nineteenth-century Lutheran and Catholic Germany. As the present Russian dissidents show, a challenge to the social order and to its religious basis in Communist ideology represent one and the same challenge.

To the modern age (despite my last remark), this religious establishment of society was believed to have ended with the criticism and the decline, and the subsequent disestablishment, of organized religion, that is to say, of the church or the churches in modern society. Now, it was believed, modern societies would enjoy a secular, a natural, a nonreligious basis: priests would vanish from chancelleries, courts, and banks, theologians from universities, and religious rites from political events—except as there might be a brief invocation and an even briefer benediction. Almost every society newly refashioned since our own revolution and that of France, except possibly Japanese fascist society in the 1930s and certainly with the present exception of Iran, has built itself deliberately on a nonreligious basis. Correspondingly, most studies of society have regarded this characteristic of traditional societies as a function of the past, that is, of their ignorance, their lack of moral and political self-consciousness, and therefore of the "immaturity" of these traditional societies.

The interesting thing to a philosopher of religion is the apparent error of this conclusion, or better, its relative incredibility in the present. I have cited contemporary social studies of modern society by Berger, Luckmann, Bellah, Parsons, Geertz, and others, who find this religious component essentially present whether the official churches have a role corresponding to that presence or not. Even more interestingly, the three major social and political powers of the present: the United States, Russia, and China—and one could make the same analysis of others—exhibit, despite their secular self-understanding, the same traits vis-à-vis a religious substance as did traditional societies. Each embodies, and sees itself as doing so, a "way of life" or a set of basic symbols which it regards as essential to its security and its well-being, to which, in various degrees, it expects each of its members to be devoted, which it seeks to increase in authority inwardly and to expand in respect and effectiveness outwardly. Each knows that its *being* as a society depends upon the credibility and the grasping power of those symbols and the life they express. And, finally, each regards this way of life, and its symbols and norms, as ultimate for history, as embodying the true worth of history, and so as expressing the true destiny of historical mankind—in sum, as providing the avenue for the realization of the fullest humanity, or, in religious language, salvation. Formally, therefore, these are "religious" societies; and their anxieties and confidence, their ultimate questions and their answers to these questions, their fanaticism and their virtues, can only be understood if we understand this religious dimension of their existence. Religion is very much a part of our social existence in the modern communities that surround us.

Thus, one answer has appeared to our first question: where in ordinary experience does (a) religious language find a common usage, and (b) where does an experience of the sacred and the ultimate make its appearance? The answer would be: religious or mythical speech appears in all contemporary political speech, and when any culture is expressing its most ultimate convictions, norms, and expectations; and the sacred is manifest most commonly to us—as to all cultures—in and through the forms, usages, and requirements of our common life.

There is one other note to make. As these two examples, America and Russia, indicate, a religious substance has not only a constitutive, establishing, conserving role in social history—illustrated in both of these two nations now that they are each firmly established—but also an important radical, upsetting, and reconstituting or transformative role in history. For whatever other factors were at work, and there were many, there was, first of all, at the base and origin of each of these societies when they were new or being formed, a cluster of primary symbols about human being, history, and society, a "not-yet" social vision that each bore, that helped to generate that new society. And, secondly, that "not-yet" symbolic vision in each case also helped to dismantle and ultimately to destroy an older world with different symbols, different structures, a different "religious substance." Thus, the religious base of society can function both conservatively and radically, creatively and destructively. Correspondingly, it is this religious dimension of cultural life that is causative of the infinity of passion and of cruelty, as of commitment, courage, and self-sacrifice, that give to history its meaning and its terror. The religious element in existence is by no means simply "good," mild, or benevolent. It is, as recent events in Iran have shown, terrifying, terrible, and demonic as well. Certainly it is always important.

A final discipline—if we can call it that—with which the philosophy of religion is concerned is the philosophy of history. But that is probably too intellectual or academic a description of what I have in mind. It is more precise to describe it as an understanding of historical process and of our relation to that process, the relation especially of our community to it—our sense of the course of history and our common group destiny or vocation within that course. This question has been of profound importance in modern self-understanding and in every modern society. The religious myths that have structured modern societies—for example, our own and that of Communist Russia—and thus that constitute their re-ligious substance as we have described that substance, have been *historical* myths, that is, myths about the character of the process of history, its shape and direction, and especially about the relation of that particular society to this ultimate course of history. It is the historical character of their myths—and the fact that they each pretend that these myths are "science"—that distinguishes modern societies from traditional ones, not the illusion that they have no myths while traditional societies did have them.

I do not think I need describe the myth about history and our relation to it that has provided the religious substance of American culture. It has been too basic to our life as a culture to require that and too deeply ingrained in all of us as the way things—history—are. Its usual name is the Myth of Progress, or belief in it. It sees history, beginning way back ⬅ with Egypt and Greece, as a story of cumulative development leading up to modern times temporally and to Western culture, and especially to America, spatially. Here and now, with us, the goal towards which this story has led, and so the goal in which it culminates, is represented by our culture. Thus, in terms of this story, do we know who we are, what we are to do, and what we can count on? This story has been one of cumulative learning and cumulative techniques, leading up to the scientific and technological world we so clearly represent. One finds it ⬅ engraved in all our grade-school textbooks in countless graphs of the number of telephones, the miles of railroads, the number of televisions, the number of cars, toilets, and so on, all of which are conceived to represent Civilization and in all of which we are clearly Number One. This is progress, and more of the same, will, we have believed, more and more "free" the future from its ills. It is also the story of the cumulative freeing of men and women from political, religious, and social authorities and tyrannies, of mankind from older brutalities and cruelty. Again, we, as the prime example of democracy, represent this culminating phase of the historical and moral development of men and women. In neither case has history completed itself: science and technology will grow indefinitely, remaking our ideas of the world and the world itself, generation after generation. Democracy will also increase, entering and transforming those areas of economics, racial, and social existence not yet freed from traditional authorities. But in any case, these developments will be more of the same thing that has found its perfect exhibition so far in our own community.

This myth, I hardly need say, has governed our common existence for some time. It helps us determine what is creative and what is not in the world, and what our own priorities are or should be. It tells us what to defend and why we defend it. It gives meaning to our work, confidence in the midst of failure, and hope in the face of tragedy or of temporary discouragement. It helps us to distinguish good from evil forces in the world around us, and gives us confidence in the ultimate victory of good over evil in history. Above all, it tells us who we are in history and why we are here. It forms the ultimate set of presuppositions for most of our aims and so our patterns of education. The sciences, the social sciences, and the humanities understand their role and worth—and large parts of their methods—on its basis; it represents the one common creed of our academic life. Like the similar Communist myth in Russia, this myth functions in our social existence "religiously," that is, as the ultimate formative and authoritative symbolic structure of our commonality. It is crucial for our effective living, our credible self-understanding, and our creative action for the future.

Now, what makes this issue of more than academic interest today—and one with which the philosophy of religion and also theology have increasingly therefore concerned themselves—is that this myth, and with it much of the substance of our cultural life, has been disintegrating around us. It is, I would suggest, the disintegration of this *secular* myth—not that of the traditional Christian mythos—that constitutes the present religious crisis of American society. For now our questions about the meaning of our work and our lives, of the significance and insignificance of what we are and do, of good and evil and the ultimate result of their encounter, that is, of the victory of the good and the conquest of the evil in history, have no framework in which to find an answer. Above all, our confidence in our own history and so ourselves as a community has been badly shaken: that confidence was based on the assurance that our science and technology were building a better world, and our growing freedoms were establishing the grounds for a fuller humanity everywhere. Of this hope in the future we are now much less sure. Science and technology seem to be capable of making the world demonic, inhuman, soulless; and freedom seems ever anew subject to some mode of historical fatedness and possibly in the end, helpless.

What we tend to call the counterculture: religiously, ethically, communally, with its religious cell groups, its "trips," its separation, and its indifference—is, various as it is, a reaction to the dispersal and disintegration of the religious substance of the wider culture, and an attempt to rediscover and reconstruct, on very simple, often esoteric, lines, a new way of being human. The main thrusts of this counterculture have been against the values, the norms, the roles, and the modes of intellectual excellence of our dominant scientific, technological, industrial, commercial, and bourgeois culture. Only secondarily has it attacked organized religion. It has seen that culture not as an area full of the promise of human fulfillment, but either, as in the radical phase, as an arena of destructive evil, or, as in the present religious phase, as neutral, necessary, but radically insufficient—a necessary base, so to speak, for the real life that is lived in meditation or contemplative groups in the ashram, whose world is alongside but not part of the wider society. Here again an answer to our first question has appeared. A use and meaning of religious language appears in ordinary "experience," but outside the wider social world, in the internal world of yogic and meditative experience, an experience which rescues the self and its reality and meaning from the outside commercial, technical, and country-club worlds that seem to make that self unreal, its work worthless, and its community relations barren.

The creative effects of these religious movements in a spiritually disintegrating culture are unquestioned, and witnessed to by countless persons. For the philosopher of religion and the theologian, a perennial question remains: is there any way the religious dimension of our social, political, and historical existence, of our society, can find a relationship and creative interaction with the religious dimension of our inward, personal existence found in these small religious communities? This is also a crucial question for our futures. If the social world is bereft of all genuine, creative, and religious substance, new demons will rush in and take over, trampling under academic, philosopher of religion, and meditator together! For as we have seen, society is religious, its politics are sacral, and left without religious criticism and concern, it can well become demonic.

3

THE DIALECTIC OF
CHRISTIAN BELIEF

I t is hardly original, though it is ironic, to point out the complexity, not to say the murkiness, of this subject: rationality and Christian belief. How intellectual clarity is related to religious conviction is itself unclear; how the mystery of faith is qualified by rationality is itself mysterious. My purpose, therefore, is not to provide a finished answer to this question; rather, as a beginning, it is to uncover some of the more important issues involved and so some of the reasons this question is itself a part of the mystery of faith. I will discuss the rationality of Christian belief instead of that of religious belief in general. The relation of rationality to religious belief takes an entirely different form in religious traditions other than Christianity (for example, in Buddhism). Our discussion will be useful only if it deals with its subject in the concrete, in relation to the issue of rationality that the particular form of Christianity poses.

At the start, it may be helpful to point out two importantly different ways the question of rationality and Christian belief arises. These two forms of the questions are at once quite distinct from each other, and yet these two distinct modes intertwine in each phase of every discussion of this theme and can, unless held distinct in the mind, breed all sorts of confusion. First, there is the relation of what can possibly be proved in the corpus of Christian faith (e.g., the theistic claim) to other aspects of the faith which cannot be proved, e.g., the incarnation, atonement, etc. If the question is posed thusly, i.e., as a relation between what is provable and what may be credible on other grounds, then rationality includes the first, provable part, and Christian belief appears as referent to that rational part *plus* all the other symbols that cannot be proved—and our question concerns the relation of these two parts to each other, a question investigated with great power by Thomas Aquinas. The question, however, of rationality and Christian belief may refer to another relation entirely, namely, that between Christianity as a total system of beliefs, what Sören Kierkegaard called Christianity as a possibility, an aesthetic system, on the one hand, and, on the other hand, Christianity as a qualification of our existence, as reflection qualifying not ideas so much as life—the integration or "reduplication" of the system (as rational, irrational, or credible) into human existence and praxis—a pair of distinctions made crystal clear by Kierkegaard.

Obviously, in this Kierkegaardian context the relation of rationality to Christian belief changes its referents: rationality now referring to the total corpus as a rational or aesthetic possibility subject to direct argument, and Christian belief (faith) referring to Christian reflection as it qualifies our existence, and thus a mode of reflection not at all subject to direct argument. I would suggest that much of the confusion associated with this problem has arisen from failing to keep these two sets of distinctions themselves distinct. Thus, for example, many have heatedly denied the possibility of a natural theology because they were conscious of the second distinction, namely, that between the requirements of rational possibility and those of religious existence; or, alternatively, many have defended the role of rational argument and of coherent system by denying as irrelevant to Christian reflection the existential element, the element of decision and commitment. On the whole, except for the last part of this study, we shall stay within the confines of the first context, namely, that which considers Christianity as an aesthetic possibility for reflection, debate, and direct argument, a possibility for decision, not the context which considers how Christianity becomes or might become a qualification of our existence.

The general issue we shall explore concerns the relation of what may be called the rational component in Christian belief to the other elements which may be believed but are not provable by reason alone—Aquinas's issue as noted above. I use the word *credible* for those other elements to indicate that although they cannot be proved by reason from general experience, they are not irrational and can in fact be defended and/or warranted by various forms of relevant argument. My main thesis is that there is a basic dialectic to be uncovered in the relation of rationality and Christian belief, a dialectic which moves from rationality through incredibility to credibility. If this be so, then the rational and the credible elements of Christian faith, while distinct in their grounds and their warrants, nevertheless are dialectically interdependent such that the rationality of the one and the credibility of the other disappears if either element is separated or isolated from the other. The same point can be put in another way: Christianity is credible only as a *total* system of symbols. While some of its essential symbols may be demonstrable in isolation, nevertheless, if they are left in isolation, they forfeit their rationality and become incredible and, *a fortiori,* irrational. Thus, while a natural theology is an integral and essential moment in the total dialectic of Christian belief, it is a part within a wider, credible whole, an aspect of the total viewpoint of faith. Its rationality, while defensible and significant, is therefore itself in the end dependent on the more elusive, less rigorous, and scarcely "natural" intelligibility and meaning characteristic of the faith as a whole. Let me now seek to make clear this thesis and to disclose its grounds, its dialectic, and the interdependence of moments within it.

Among the many areas where this thesis may be illustrated, the historical character of our being, both individual and social, is one of the most useful. For Christianity in its Scriptures and in most, if not all, of its theological formulations concerns itself with both the structure and the meaning of our historical being, and obviously many of our own deepest existential and religious issues arise in relation to our historicity. Finally, not insignificant to my proposal, I have been pondering the relation of Christianity to historicity for some time. Now, our own question enters because when one analyzes the synchronic structure of our temporal being, a number of convincing arguments appear for positing a divine ground and context for that being. Thus does the theistic claim arise and does Christianity receive its essential component of "rationality," the natural theological base for all else that is affirmed. On the other hand, the human experience of the diachronic character of its historical being, either as an individual or as a member of a historical group, has indicated—as often as not—that that historical being is alienated and estranged, immersed in a destiny that is chaotic, incoherent, and grimly determined or fated for suffering, and faced with possibilities that are menacing and destructive as much as they are creative. The structure of our historical being leads to the claim that temporal finitude has its source in a divine creative ground; yet the character of our concrete historical existence as estranged and alienated continually can and does obscure that divine ground in conflict, meaninglessness, suffering, and despair. The result is that at that point *deus* becomes radically *absconditus,* and the theistic claim begins now to seem incredible and the arguments that ground it irrational. The concrete reality of historical being as both temporal and estranged now challenges the rationality and meaningfulness of finite existence, the sense of the reality of God, and as a consequence the rationality of religious or of Christian belief.

Ironically, however, it is also precisely at that point that the deeper relevance of the theistic claim appears for the first time, and the real significance of the divine ground—and of belief—enters. For in relation to our estrangement, the divine, obscured now as ground, manifests itself as redemptive. This redemptive movement, as we would all surely agree, represents both the center of Christian witness and the basis of whatever ultimate importance Christian belief may have. Finally, this redemptive presence of the divine in grace—in new insight and new life—is by the nature of the case not "rational" in the above sense. It is not present in the analyzable essential structure of historical being. It is given to it in answer to the warping and self-destruction of that structure. It is at best credible, not "rational"—but without that credibility based on redemptive grace, the rationaity of theism which is its foundation is itself subverted, just as without the rational foundation with which we began, the credibility of the articles of grace is dissolved.

A dialectic essential to the character of Christian belief has appeared that has had confusing reverberations all through the history of Christian reflection. Catholicism has clearly recognized these two separable but interrelated moments, but—to my mind—integrated them wrongly in terms of the two levels of nature and of grace, a structure almost inconceivable to the modern historical consciousness. Protestantism rightly challenged that structure but tended itself to overlook the dialectic. The result has been that it either took the second and third moments as decisive, i.e., estrangement, incredibility, and kerygma, or it took only the first as decisive, natural theology, and a "natural" grace. In a way, of course, both are right and yet both also wrong.

Seemingly, if we would establish the legitimacy—the rationality—of the theistic underpinning of a Christian interpretation of life, we must emphasize historical being's ontological structure as good, intelligible, and meaningful, and through that structure the relation to a divine ground, i.e., a philosophical theism. But, by the same token, such an emphasis on the first moment's possibility almost by necessity regards history's self-contradiction and tragedy, its warping and obscuring of that structure and its overwhelming need of grace, as subversive of rationality. If, on the other hand, we would proclaim the relevance and legitimacy of the redemptive side of a Christian interpretation of life, we must emphasize the contradictions apparent in history's actuality and the incredibility of grace—and so obscure the reality and intelligibility of the God who purports to redeem. A natural theology seems to miss, or be in danger of doing so, the actual or concrete character of history's life, and to make irrelevant the message of the redemption it seeks rationally to defend. A purely kerygmatic Christianity, aware of evil and centered in the surprising gift of grace, seems either to undermine its own ontological and theological foundations or else to assert at the end an ultimate coherence and rationality it so vigorously denied at its inception. The dialectical interdependence—my initial thesis—of the rational and the credible parts of the Christian corpus is here illustrated. On the one hand, no redemptive possibilities are fully rational or even credible unless their grounds are rationally coherent with the essential structure of our beings; on the other hand, concrete existence makes the very rationality of theism incredible unless the reality of redemptive grace is found in some way credible.

This is, I suspect, the reason that the arguments of natural theology, its component of rationality, appear to be "rational" only to those who find the remainder of Christian affirmation credible. Christian belief is based rationally on a philosophical analysis of our finitude; but that very rationality is itself dependent, granted the estrangement of the actuality of our existence and the consequent hiddenness of God, on the credibility of the other elements of Christian belief which cannot be so demonstrated. There is a dialectic of rationality, incredibility, and credibility that constitutes the formal structure of Christian belief, with the negative, estrangement, initiating the movement from one moment to the other. If these moments are separated, each one loses its status, and Christianity dissolves as a total interpretation of life. If they are not distinguished, then untold confusion results. If they are held in distinction and yet tension, then rationality and credibility join to make intelligible the incredible grace and promise which Christian faith proclaims.

In order to explore this dialectic of rationality, incredibility, and credibility further, let us look more closely at the character of historical being in order to see more clearly the initial rationality of theism, the effects on that rationality of estrangement, and the final moment of what may be called the credibility of an incredible grace.

An ontological analysis of our finitude reveals, I believe, that that finitude is most basically to be characterized as temporal or in process, and that the structure of that process is one of destiny—a given from our immediate past and that of our world—in union with freedom or self-actualization. Such an ontological structure can be shown to be the presupposition of our experience of ourselves and of the history in which we are immersed, of social and political life, and, finally, of those who study history and seek to understand it—be they historians, social scientists, futurologists, or philosophers, and however much they may deny the presence of such ontological presuppositions or scorn inquiry into them. Now, the point is that while this ontological structure makes possible the openness, the contingency, and the "fallenness" of history— and thus opens the door to history's disorder, irrationality, and meaninglessness as well as to its creativity—nevertheless, it itself entails a deeper, necessary, all-encompassing ground as the condition of its possibility. This entailment is present in all three phases of temporal passage: the relation of past destiny to present, the self-actualization of the present out of that destiny and novel possibility, and the relation of future possibility to present. We cannot here give more than an outline of these arguments; intimations of one or another of them are to be found in Augustine, Aquinas, Calvin, Schleiermacher, Tillich, and especially Whitehead.

If finite being be temporal, in process, then it is characterized by radical passingness, the vanishing of what has just become, the relative nonbeing of what has been actual. This characteristic of temporal being, that the past fades and only the present is real, makes possible both creative freedom and the new; its shadow side is the loss of the immediate past, its disappearance into relative unreality and ineffectiveness. But one of the mysteries of time is that the achieved past is nevertheless effective. It forms the destiny for each present, providing it with its continuing reality, shaping in part its form, and thus making possible "substances" or enduring entities, causality, experience, and cognition. All relations, continuity, order, and thus all life itself depend on the effectiveness in the arising present of a past which, if being be temporal, has vanished into relative nonbeing. Thus, entailed in the relation of the past that is gone to a present made and made itself by that past is the presence of a deeper, creative ground, a ground that does not pass away but brings each achieved and objectified past into the creative present as the latter's formative destiny, its initial data, the origin of its thrownness and its facticity. The ground of the contingent, self-actualizing present, and so of all secondary causality and cognition, is, as Augustine and Aquinas both said, a primary causality that is not contingent but necessary, or as Whitehead terms it, a "creativity" out of which new occasions arise. This is what the classical tradition in theology has called the first work of providence, "the preservation of the creature over time." Such a timeless divine work in time is directly entailed by the radical temporality of all creaturely being.

➤ The past forms in large part the present—but never completely. In history, however much all seems determined by destiny, there is always a response that is creative of the actual event. Thus does freedom, the principle of self-actualization, enter historical process; each occcasion is in part *causa sui,* else all be determined and novelty be as unreal as would be intentions, decisions, errors and sin. If this be so, then another "mystery" in the midst of passage has appeared, namely, the deeper ground of freedom itself. For ipso facto the power to be and to be free cannot arise either from the past or even from given possibility—else there be no *self*-actualization. And as Schleiermacher points out, our experience of freedom is not an experience of originating our freedom. As Augustine and Aquinas reiterate, the power of all secondary causality is a *given,* not a self-created, power—and by its nature not given by any creaturely reality behind or ahead of us. Thus, again there is entailed in the character of passage, this time in that of the self-actualizing present, a deeper, necessary, creative divine ground from which each occasion as self-formative arises; this is the second, "concurring" work of providence, whereby freedom comes to be in each historical event.

Finally, there is no temporal event without the impingement on it of future and so of novel possibility—as Whitehead, Heidegger, Ernst Bloch, and the eschatologists have reminded us. Not only novelty but also openness, genuine alternatives, and thus freedom depend on this effective presence of real possibility to each self-actualizing present. But, as Whitehead has shown, possibilities to be, and to be effective "must be somewhere," related to actuality, for only actuality can provide an effective reason for anything actual. And in a world characterized by self-actualizing freedom as well as open possibility, possibilities must be primordially graded into a relevant order if they are to help fashion an orderly actuality. Thus, there must be a primordial actuality that includes in its envisionment all of possibility as possible, setting those novel forms into a relevant order and thus providing the ontological ground for novelty, openness, and freedom in experience. Novelty in the midst of continuing order characterizes our experience of temporal being; such experience is unintelligible without a divine ground, both of continuity and of freedom, and now of relevant possibility. This is the third and final ontological role of providence, as "directing" passage through its eternal envisionment of relevant possibilities for the changing flux.

In all three of its phases, temporal being requires some ground beyond temporality and yet actively within it: as the continuing source of the destiny from the immediate past, as the ground of present self-actualization, and as the creative "place" of future possibility. Those aspects of the structure of temporal being that have originally seemed to challenge the rationality of theism—the relative nonbeing of time, the freedom of temporal being, and the unlimited openness of new possibilities—far from denying theism, require it rationally. Rationality is deeply characteristic of the most fundamental claim of Christian faith about the reality and effectiveness of God in historical passage.

The ontological structure of historical being, then, proclaims the rationality of theism. It is, however, also true that the concrete character of historical actuality deeply challenges the rationality of that theistic claim. For the actuality of historical existence is estranged from this structure of destiny, freedom, and creative possibility. Creative destiny, freedom, and open possibility appear, to be sure, in much historical experience, for such experience would not be possible without them; and many epochs of history, for example, the period of early modernity, experienced this meaningful and creative side of history as history's predominant character. Nevertheless, to other periods and to those groups and classes which are not dominant, historical passage manifests a different, grimmer, and less creative face. At such times and for such groups, destiny is in union neither with freedom nor with possibility. Rather the "given" from the historical past, embodied in warped institutions, chaotic events, and twisted characters, appears as Fate, as a given which crushes freedom and is void of genuine and creative possibility. Here the ontological structure of history is warped, fallen—or, in Tillich's word, estranged. This is an objective, though not necessitated, characteristic of historical being, not merely an inward psychological or existential quality. For the injustice of institutional forms is objective; historical conflicts are objective; and the disorder and suffering that result are no mere psychological matters, as surely as the nemesis awaiting each warped civilization is as objective, and more concrete, than any economic graph. At such times, moreover, the ontological structure of history as destiny, freedom, and possibility is radically obscured. Destiny has become fate; freedom is bound within evil choices or arbitrary and ineffective spasms; and creative possibilities seem unreal. Obviously, at such times and from such a perspective, the theistic claim, based on a structure that is estranged from itself and now obscured, itself appears as ungrounded, irrational, and even oppressive.

Heralding a destiny that is really fate, theism appears as an ideology blessing the dubious status quo; proclaiming a freedom that is in fact oppressed, it appears as unrealistic idealism; in promising possibilities that seem impossible, it seems delusory, an opiate. The estrangement of the structure of historical being makes incredible the rational implications of that essential structure. And because religion itself participates fully in that estrangement, its very rationality, persuasiveness, and promise can become demonic, themselves a part of the warped character of historical life—as most social revolutionaries have rightly felt. As we noted, in the face of the warped actuality of history, the rational component of faith, descriptive of the essential structure of passage but not of its fallen concreteness, becomes either a pious and ineffective abstraction or a demonic ideology, incredible to eyes fastened on the concreteness of history's actuality.

Profound theology has had much to say about the *deus absconditus*. The sources of this negative symbol in the experience of fatedness, meaninglessness, suffering, and judgment are evident. For the actuality of historical experience is filled with all of these, and it follows that the creative providence of God as we have described it is surely there neither experienced nor known. In these brief remarks on this theme, I would like to dwell more on the basis in the ontological structure of passage for this radical hiddenness—the incredibility of God—than on the phenomenological or ontic description of the estrangement of history. Any contemporary assessment of the social present and immediate prospects of our technological, nationalistic, and capitalistic society will fill in the latter.

The relation of ontological structure to its estrangement is of course exceedingly close. Because of the structure as freedom, the estrangement is possible; and because of the estrangement, the structure is obscured. This is the deepest ground, relevant at least to philosophical inquiry and to "rationality," of what we have called the incredibility of theism, though, as noted, the qualitative, ontic character of a warped history in conflict, injustice, suffering, and meaninglessness also provides ample ground for an existential incredibility.

We have pictured the creative work of providence as providing that continuing unity of past, present, and future that makes an event possible, and that is therefore the ontological condition for temporal being, being in process. Thus, through the work of God is nonbeing overcome and temporal finitude emerges: achieved actuality is brought as creative destiny into the present as the condition of the continuity of being and of structure; self-actualization emerges as formative of that destiny in the light of presented alternatives; and future possibilities are presented as novel and creative options to this complex of past and present. When, however, the relation of the emerging event to its divine ground is transformed in estrangement, this creative structure, while not lost—or else temporal finitude would cease to be—is warped. The unity of past, present, and future created and upheld by providence is broken, and historical actuality takes on that new character made familiar by phenomenological analyses of sin, conflict, meaninglessness, and despair. Now the past is either lost, making the present empty of reality, or it becomes an all-determining fate that crushes the present and the future. With its divine ground obscured, freedom loses touch with its own destiny, and so with itself—and the present entity faces self-negation or self-elevation. Overwhelmed by contingency or fatedness in the given and in itself, freedom despairs of its roles in self- and in world creation. And possibility, no longer related creatively to destiny, appears as arbitrary, orderless, and unreal. Sin results, ontologically and experientially, in the loss of the unity of past, present, and future: the vanishing of the past into inaccessible unreality, the smothering of the present as determined by fate, and the closing of the future as bereft of possibility. In each phase of temporality, unreality and nonbeing—and suffering— dominate our individual and social existence.

Under such circumstances, historical existence—and the individual lives immersed in it—appears as fated, meaningless, and suffused with suffering and guilt; and philosophical reflection finds only these as the essential character of what it scrutinizes. Let us note that even the immanent ontological structure of temporal finitude—as destiny, freedom, and possibility—is *"absconditus."* Thus, *a fortiori,* its divine ground disappears and "is silent." This is why in epochs dominated by a sense of estrangement rather than of essential structure, a rationally "incredible" providence becomes, through faith, the *only* basis for confidence in that essential structure, in destiny, freedom, and possibility as foundational to all finite being—as the examples of Augustine and Calvin so clearly show. In any case, on the ontological as well as on the ontic descriptive level of analysis, the negative moment of the dialectic, estrangement, seems at this point to overwhelm the positive thesis constituting the rationality of theistic providence and to make the latter incredible. And let us further note, if this analysis be correct, that the more the historical or process character of finite being be emphasized, the more the effects of estrangement on the cognition of the divine ground, as well as on the power of the human will, will of necessity be emphasized—for it is only eternity that holds the moments of our time together, and a radically temporal process without the divine ground tends to fall apart and to reveal nothing of God.

If, as Karl Barth says, it be Catholic to emphasize a natural theology, and if it be Protestant to emphasize the effects of sin on the possibility of the knowledge of God—though both assertions must be carefully qualified—we have in the pursuit of our theme uncovered a dialectical interpretation of *both* the Catholic and the Protestant moments. The structural foundation of Christian faith, the theistic claim that there is a divine ground to historical passage, can be rationally argued from the ontological structure of passage. However, as I have just shown, both that structure and its ground become obscured by the concrete actuality of historical existence. In this situation, not only does that rationality become irrational—or incredible—but by making it central to the statement of the faith, the concreteness of historical life can be overlooked, the deepest relevance of the gospel forgotten, and the faith turned into a pious abstraction unrelated to existential concreteness or, as noted, a dangerous ideology too much related to the divinely given. On the other hand, those further symbolic elements of the faith that describe, judge, and seek to resolve this estrangement through the witness to redemption, i.e., the law and the gospel, have no meaning and structure, and surely no intelligibility, without this original theistic foundation. As Irenaeus and Tertullian argued against the Gnostics, God cannot be judge and redeemer unless God is also creator of all and sovereign lord of historical passage; the gospel of redemption is scarcely credible without the radical foundation of theism. Thus are the two elements with which we began—the rational and the credible elements—interrelated because of the incredible but real intervening moment of estrangement that makes each in its own way in turn "incredible." Estrangement makes a rational theism *rationally* incredible as most of intellectual modernity avers; and it makes the appearance of redemption *existentially* incredible, unexpected, unmerited, the marks of the presence of grace. So thoroughly does estrangement overturn the fundamental structure of things, that the same negation that makes theism incredible also gives the most essential quality of God, the divine love, the paradoxicality and incredibility of grace.

Let me close this brief discussion of the dialectic of rationality, incredibility, and credibility by making further explicit why I speak of credibility and what I mean by it. It should be clear by now that there are two major reasons for the distinction I have drawn between rationality and credibility. The first is the more formal reason that, as already noted, a large part of the content of Christian belief concerns matters not derivable directly from the ontological structure of our finitude and so not entailed by even the most careful and systematic rational or empirical scrutiny of that structure. Estrangement, if the Christian view of it be correct, is a warping through freedom of that structure, not a necessary consequence of it; it cannot, therefore, be "proved" by means of a systematic delineation of that structure—for "proof" involves uncovering the necessary connections of an assumed aspect of an ontological structure with other aspects. It is for this reason that metaphysical descriptions of existence always appear abstract in relation to the concreteness of existence: either they outline its essential structure and miss its actual estrangement, or they depict its estrangement, take that for the essential structure, and so miss the creative elements within it. In any case, if rationality connotes what can be philosophically demonstrated—and that has been my use of the term—then only the theistic component is "rational" in that sense, and the symbolic descriptions of estrangement and of its resolution in grace remain beyond the scope of rationality so defined.

The second reason is closely associated with the first but is more existential. As noted earlier, concrete existence is a mixture of creative, essential elements: destiny, freedom, and possibility, and within them the work of providence, on the one hand, with aspects of estrangement, fatedness, self-destruction, and meaninglessness on the other. Since in historical being this mixture arises not out of necessity but out of the compound of destiny and freedom, its character, the balance of the two contrasting components, is at each moment undecided, as is its ultimate issue. Thus is history a diachronic drama and not a synchronic logical or entailed system, a drama whose ultimate intelligibility and meaning is at each moment both partly manifest and partly obscured. Unintelligibility as well as intelligibility, mystery as well as meaning, are ingredients in the concreteness of personal and historical being. No clear vision of either the structure, the pattern, or the outcome of this drama is thus possible from within its midst. If such an overall pattern is presumed, it will be, as noted, at best an abstraction from this duality, a premature closing of the contest, and at worst an assignation of meaning from one partial viewpoint and therefore ideological. All total visions, therefore, and Christianity is one of them, are held as much by faith as by persuasive insight—though both grounds are there. And all of them must, if they are to be self-critical of their own ideological temptations and pretensions, recognize essentially this inability to grasp the whole with demonstrable certainty and objective clarity. Though ontology has a vital role in the understanding of history, any comprehension of history as a whole, and so any theological understanding, has the form of a global "myth" and not of a systematic ontology; and such total views are, as Calivin said, more matters of confidence than of certainty. If Christian belief as a total view does not recognize its own status as credible rather than demonstrable ("scientific," as the Marxists say of theirs), it will, as has often happened, appear more as an abstract idealism or as a pretentious idolatry than as a healing grasp of a mystery beyond any clear and definitive comprehension.

The existential meaninglessness resulting from estrangement penetrates deeply, moreover, into the formal possibility of theism as rational. For, as we have noted, in the case of each phase of temporal being that formal possibility depends upon a metaphysical inference, namely, that if it is to be intelligibly understood, finitude must be understood as created, upheld, and guided by a divine ground. But the possibility, legitimacy, and meaningfulness of such an inference can itself be questioned, as much contemporary philosophy has done. The reason for this questionableness is that such inferences beyond the given, i.e., beyond the immediate reality of destiny, of freedom, and of possibility, presuppose that being is throughout characterized by rationality, that being is *logos* as well as power, else logic and the language of inference have no relevance beyond empirical verification. If this be so, then a deep cultural or personal experience of estrangement and therefore of the irrationality and meaninglessness of historical being can in turn obscure this intuition of the logos of being and render the foundations of theistic rationality, i.e., the possibility of metaphysical inference, ungrounded and problematic. An intuition of fundamental order, itself no more than credible, grounds and establishes the possibility of metaphysical inference and of theistic rationality. Its preservation in the midst of estrangement can depend—though in buoyant ages it does not—on the credibility of religious faith as a whole—which is why natural theology today tends to prosper in seminaries, religious groups, and among their representatives, however "purely rational" or "purely philosophical" it may seek to present itself.

To say that the total system of Christian symbols is not rational in the sense of philosophically demonstrable is not, however, to maintain that it is irrational. For it is, as I have argued, credible: it can satisfy the mind as a valid symbolic thematization of the totality of concrete experience as no other global viewpoint can. As many contemporaries have urged, the criteria of its credibility are coherence among its major symbolic elements and adequacy to the contours of concrete experience taken as a whole. One can also add that its own theological requirements are "appropriate," that is, faithful to the symbolic tradition within Scripture and the historical interpretation of the Christian community.

The tricky word in this formula is, of course, adequacy. How does one show that a particular point of view is adequate to the general contours of experience if it be granted that that viewpoint cannot be "proved" from experience? Obviously, the answer is that the symbols which are said to be adequate must be shown to "fit" the shape of the experience they claim adequately to thematize. But the difficulty is that what that shape is taken to be—what are to me "the facts"—is itself in significant part determined by the symbolic structure with which experience is interpreted, and there is no uninterpreted experience. Thus is there what has been called the "theological circle" in relation to all foundational symbolic systems; and thus are arguments about adequacy—when one is considering interpretations of personal, historical, or social being as a whole—inevitably circular and inconclusive, each debater bringing forth not only a different symbolic complex but also a different constellation of common facts to prove the adequacy of that complex.

Despite these difficulties, however, I believe it can be shown that a

Christian interpretation provides a clearer, more illuminative, and more complete access to the full character of personal and historical experience than any other viewpoint. Its symbols together make intelligible our existence by depicting its contours accurately, by omitting or glossing over none of the negative or counterfactual aspects of that existence, and by providing grounds for those forms of human existence and of action that fulfill human potentialities rather than shrink them. It leads to illumination, courage, and creative praxis, and thus is it credible. Where proof is not possible, it is, as Kierkegaard said, nevertheless important for reason to show *why* demonstration is here not possible; and, I have added, it is important to establish the fullest level of credibility, namely, that of coherence and adequacy, as an intellectual warrant for the viewpoint that is to be believed. This theology can and must do— for nothing is believed that is also not thought by the mind to be true, that is not held to be credible.

One further word on the conditions and character of credibility. Since, I have argued, the rationality of Christian belief is itself dialectically intertwined with its incredibility and its credibility, it seems to me to follow that both that rational component and the credible component are themselves dependent—if either one is to be credible—on what we might call *intimations in experience* of the full scope of Christian faith. It has been argued—by myself and others—that the rationality of the theistic claim appears as rational only to those who are aware of or open to a dimension of ultimacy and sacrality in their own existence which that rational component seeks to explicate conceptually. And we have here made the further point that the rationality of metaphysical inference is itself grounded in a deep "religious" intuition of being as logos. Now, if we take our thesis of interdependence seriously—and the point that theism may well be irrational and certainly incredible to one caught in and overwhelmed by estrangement—it follows that Christian theism is "rational" only to those who also have intuitions of the estrangement of life, on the one hand, and of its possibilities of healing despite that estrangement, on the other, i.e., to those who have intimations of both sin and grace, though they surely do not need explicitly either to know or to affirm those symbols. Experience and the intellectual interpretation of experience are correlative categories and go together if they go at all. If, then, it is the total credibility of the Christian viewpoint that helps to give rationality to its rational component, then those experiences of estrangement and of rescue, of new possibilities in a seemingly fated situation—however unthematized into Christian symbols these intimations may be—are essential conditions for the whole dialectic if it is to reach its term in belief.

In conclusion, I would urge that Kierkegaard's caveat not be forgotten in discussing rationality and belief. I have concentrated on Christianity as a system of concepts: rational, incredible, and credible, as an intellectual "possibility" for our existence. I have not considered the deeper existential questions of the conditions for its reduplication into our existence, as a thought-form qualifying our life—nor how that relation in turn qualifies its credibility for us. It seems to me that these difficult questions—bracketed so far—cannot be totally set aside. If theism be considered valid, a participating sense of the working of the divine in our existence is an element in that sense of validity; if estrangement be taken seriously as a symbol, then a consciousness of sin in ourselves and our own is its necessary condition; if the gospel of redemption be considered credible, then experience of its reality, commitment to its demands and promises, and enactment of its implications in praxis are each intimately and immediately involved. Christianity is also a series of ideas set into symbolic terms, and it can be considered, criticized, defended, and reshaped in that light. But the relevance, meaning, and validity of those symbols appear only if those symbols communicate through themselves the presence of the divine, and if they are reduplicated in enactment and in existence and not just in aesthetic possibility. For these reasons, the term *credible* takes on deeper dimensions than merely rational coherence and experiential adequacy. It becomes the important intellectual side, the side of the mind, of faith and love as the deepest qualifications of our existence as a whole—which is, after all, what both rationality and belief are all about.

4

THE POLITICAL DIMENSIONS
OF THEOLOGY

If one concentrates on basic motifs rather than on theological language, there seems to be the same deep split in our day as there was half a century ago between an individual and a social interpretation of the Christian religion: between a committed, personal, existential concentration on inward sin, grace, and reconciliation issuing in a new individual relation to God, on the one hand, and, on the other hand, an earnest, courageous concentration on the outer, the social, the political, on liberation within the customs and institutions of outward life and the impersonal relations of society, issuing in a new, objective social order in the future. Now, the deepest substantive question of current theology is, I believe, the mediation of this false opposition, an opposition untrue both to Scripture and to an adequate theological interpretation of history and of human destiny. The overcoming of this split is also crucial for our common social being. It is important that the religious and moral forces, such as they are, of our communities become integrated creatively into our common political life, not only so that Christianity may be an inspiring and shaping factor in social reform and reconstruction, but also that it may help mitigate those real possibilities, lying as well in our future, of *our* participation in social oppression and social disintegration.

My argument will be that as individual and social cannot be separated in ordinary, secular life, so they cannot be separated in religious existence. Thus, our sin, our faith, and our obedience are as constitutive of a social situation or a social history as they are of a personal, individual situation or history. Consequently, the major symbols of Christian faith relevant to these issues, God and the divine action, human nature and its remaking, sin, grace, and Kingdom, unite rather than separate the individual and the social, the personal and the historical.

I shall begin, if Karl Barth will forgive me, with some anthropological reflections on this theme—though I might as well have begun with my next point, the interpretation of the same themes in the Hebrew Scriptures. If we look at human social existence through the eyes of the most perceptive social scientists, we see emphasized two points that we shall presuppose and illustrate rather than demonstrate. The first is the interdependence of the individual and her or his social community. It is out of the community, its ways, language, norms, roles, and viewpoints on the world that each individual arises, becomes a self, and becomes fulfilled. And it is in the community—some community of common interest and aims—that the individual's creative role in life is played out and to which her or his work contributes. Part of our historicity is that we are individual selves—however unique that individuality may be—in social community and thus in history. Individual and community dance together down the corridor of time and so together they exist *coram Deo,* in the presence of God. Taken for granted in ancient cultures—Chinese, Hellenic, Hebrew, Japanese—the truth of this interpretation of individual and community is now a major theme, if not discovery, of any contemporary social science.

My second anthropological-sociological premise is that the social matrix within which we arise and have our human being has a religious dimension, as Paul Tillich liked to say, a "religious substance"—or also subsists, like its individual components, *coram Deo.* Social existence involves and depends on a shared consciousness, a shared system of meanings. This shared system of meanings is structured by symbols that shape or express the understanding of reality, of space and time, of human being and its authenticity, of life and its goods, of appropriate relations, roles, customs, and behavior, symbols which together constitute the unique gestalt, the identity or uniqueness, of that social group. To be a member of any community is to be aware of, to participate in, and to be oneself shaped, energized, and directed by this common symbolic mythos. It is, as Hegel said, to share inwardly the *Geist* of the community, its religious substance.

The "religious" character or quality of this shared mythos constitutive of a community's being can be seen from a multitude of perspectives.

An example is the commonly recognized fact that the group (say, the nation in our day) evokes with ease religious emotions of devotion, commitment, loyalty, self-sacrifice, that it quickly becomes under pressure our "ultimate concern." This religious quality of social bodies is one of the puzzling "facts" about human social existence; it requires, I believe, a theological interpretation to be made intelligible. The security of a community—perhaps the most ultimate of its ultimate concerns—is continually rendered questionable by the passage of time. That is to say, the status of a group is continually shaken by the contingency of its life and the openness, the uncontrollability, of its future. Consequently, each group stands in each new moment under the threat of fate, of being unable to control its own course and to secure its own existence. The group, so to speak, must call on the gods, or superhuman sacral powers, to deal with the problem of its own contingency in time. Now, political existence is the point where the group unites itself to steer this course through time, to secure its existence, to defend itself against this threat of Fate. Thus is the political life of any people characterized by ultimacy and by sacrality, by sacral rulers given their crucial role by the gods, by a divinely legitimated rule; and this rule will be considered legitimate only because it expresses and is in touch with, is an agent of, the fundamental grain, pattern, or sovereignty of history. No king but was in the end divinely established; no ruler but sought and received the blessing of communal religion.

The eighteenth century saw clearly this essential relation of religion, privilege, and monarchy, and the nineteenth the relation of religion and society's oppressive superstructure; but both thought that it had been a conspiracy of organized religion, especially of Christianity, that had imported this religious dimension into a potentially secular and therefore innocent politics. The twentieth century has shown, on the contrary, that ideology, a religious interpretation of and allegiance to a community's social mythos, springs up inexorably in all politics, that the divine legitimation of rule and the sacral character of a way of life—whether it be a Marxist or a liberal, capitalist ideology—is as much a character of advanced contemporary societies as was the union of religion, myth, and kingship in a traditional society—though, ironically, each of the twentieth century's religious/political myths claims to be "scientific."

The same analysis showing the dimension of ultimacy and sacrality in social existence could be made of the meanings in a culture's life that generate and permeate activity in the world by its people, and of the norms by which a people live. The social myths or ethos that make our common life possible have a religious dimension. This is the source of the community's creativity, courage, and confidence; it is also the ground of the demonic in historical life: of blind fanaticism, of infinite arrogance, of imperial ambition, of unlimited cruelty, and of ultimate violence. Even a "secular" analysis of social existence, therefore, uncovers a religious dimension in historical life. This dimension is as yet vague and undefined, the base alike of a community's creativity and of its demonic possibilities. In such an empirical uncovering, the real source or referent of this religious dimension, its ontological roots, are as yet undiscovered and undelineated. And surely any sort of resolution of its stark ambiguity of creativity and of the satanic is as yet unmanifest. All we know through social inquiry is that the religious dimension is very much there; that it is very important, if not crucial, for the life or being of the community; and that it is clearly the main source of history's capacity for suffering and for nemesis.

I will not argue that either Émile Durkheim or Tillich—and surely not Peter Berger!—are to be found full-blown in the Hebrew Scriptures' view of society or of history. However, I do believe—as I shall argue more fully in the following chapter—that there one does encounter an interpretation of history in terms of Yahweh's actions and purposes with his people that, so to speak, gives helpful clues to the ultimate grounds for these empirical social facts, that sets these evident facts into an intelligible theological, in this case ontological and anthropological, framework. In these Scriptures, the central creative act of Yahweh, the ground and prototype for the later affirmation of his creation of the cosmos itself, was his creation in history of his people Israel. The main "story" of the initial books is the story of Yahweh's calling of his people and his promises to them; of his mighty acts (as we fondly used to call them) by which this people's identity and existence were established in and through certain historical events; and of his constitution of the structure of moral and customary behavior, the norms of the community through the divine law. Let us note, moreover, that not only are what we would call the "symbolic structure of the community," its "mythos" concerning the nature of reality, authentic human and social existence, and the norms required to realize that existence given by Yahweh; also its particular economic and political structures are regarded as his work. The judges that in the beginning rescue, sustain, and guide the people; and then—though there were variant views and traditions here—the monarchical order of Israel's later life were both regarded as the work of Yahweh. In short, while they propound no social theory of community as possessing a religious dimension or substance, the Hebrew Scriptures regarded the community of Israel as divinely established or founded, and its norms of life, its structures of political rule, and its views of reality as aspects of the creative gift of Yahweh to his people in history. The frequently reviled view of Paul that "the powers that be are ordained of God" is not only intelligible sociology, it is excellent exegesis: social community, social mores and norms, and economic and political structures have a sacral foundation and a sacral status. They are essential as providing a dwelling place for humans in history; without them we can neither be nor be human.

In any case, it is clear that according to the Hebrew Scriptures, Yahweh established through creative historical activity not only a religious people or community, a kind of prototype of the church; God also established a social community, a prototype of the worldly, the secular community; and that as in modern sociology and anthropology, the two are intertwined and interdependent, the Hebrew religion existing within a social and historical abode, and society having a religious center or substance. Surely there can be no doubt that the important later symbols of the New Covenant people, the messianic reign, and even the Kingdom itself repeat and develop, rather than abrogate, this union of the social and the religious, the historical and the ideal, which begins here in the original calling and establishment of the people of God. This interrelation and interdependence of the religious and the social, the individual and the communal—and the providential constitution of both—was reexpressed in classical, Hellenic form in Augustine's *De Civitate Dei,* and variously—and often unfortunately—in the subsequent concepts of Holy Christendom and in the Calvinistic views of the Holy Community. However, later, more spiritual (more individualistic and bourgeois?) periods took this union in the Old Testament of the socio-historical with the religious as a "material" type or foretaste of the purely spiritual ecclesia and Kingdom of Christ—referred to in the New Testament—and the division between the religious and social we now seek to heal was carried forward.

The biblical basis for a religious interpretation of culture, a view which sees the mythos and the political structures of community established by providence and thus as sacral, has hardly been a popular theme in recent biblical theology. It seems replete with all the wrong overtones: with a divine emperor, with Billy Graham for breakfast, with conservative politics, and conservative, if not priestly, religion. Thus we think of valid religion, especially ethical religion, as primarily, if not exclusively, *critical* or *revolutionary* in its role in the social order. I would suggest that the Hebrew Scriptures are well aware of these dangers and speak frequently of them without denying my present point, namely, the sacral character of social tradition, of law, of mores, and of kingship in Israel's life. After all, how can we understand theologically a retrieval of social symbols unless the latter have also arisen out of the divine providential activity? The point these critics forget is the dialectical character of the Hebrew and Christian understanding of history.

As we all know, in Genesis the good creation neither nullifies nor prevents the demonic misuse by men and women of the gifts of creation; nor does the horror of the fall or of a fallen history negate the reality of the good creation. In the same way, the historical creation through providence of the symbolic meanings and structures of culture does not nullify or prevent their subsequent misuse—nor does it in any way compromise the sharp prophetic critique of the immoral character of Israel's life. Sin enters Israel's life—even the life of the chosen people granted the divine law by grace—as it had once entered an enchanted Eden. In fact, as I have intimated, it was the historical experience of the providential creation of the covenant people in conjunction with their own human misuse of the divine covenant that probably lay in back of the dialectic of creation and fall expressed in Genesis 1–3. Here, a vivid historical and social experience *coram Deo* of divine creation and of human fall is universalized into a story explanatory of the same dialectic in all of historical and social life. In any case, Israel was vividly aware in her historical experience that the gifts of providence to her had been ignored, betrayed, warped, and disfigured; the satanic had appeared in history and with it had come or was to come empirically a historical destruction, breakdown, and nemesis, and a divine rejection and judgment. This Old Testament theme of the rejection of the covenant and so the rejection of the covenant people is, except for its enactment by the Jews, notable for its absence in Christian self-understanding both in relation to the ecclesia on the one hand, and to Christendom and the Christian nations on the other. None of the latter, despite the clear historical evidence, seem ever to have thought that they too might have betrayed their own covenantal gifts.

In the study following this one, I shall attempt to give a fuller account of the view of sin or estrangement in the Hebrew Scriptures. That this symbol expresses or points to Israel's experiences of her own history from beginning to end there can be little doubt. There is hardly a moment in that history when Israel or her kings—despite their sacral gifts and status—are not doing "what is evil in the sight of Yahweh"; surely this is also our own experience of our own history, replete as it is with vast gifts of nature, freedom, new opportunity, a "new covenant"—but also repeated ambiguity and betrayal. There are two aspects of the Old Testament view of evil which may be helpful to one interested in political theology or theological politics.

The first is what Gerhard von Rad calls the early view of evil and its consequences characteristic of the Old Testament. Here, a sinful deed is regarded as having objective social consequences, even more menacing and fatal to others than to the doer of the deed, that is, to other members of his group, to his children, and to his children's children. As we know, this view was regarded by liberal commentators, anxious to show that the mature Old Testament represented nothing but the highest modern ideals, as itself immoral and "primitive." It well may have been both immoral and primitive; but, unfortunately, it was also true. And in a strange way it represents a most profound and helpful understanding of the processes of social history. In trying to give this view a modern theological interpretation, we shall find another entry, so to speak, into the relation of theology to the political, another base for a gospel that is social.

As I have argued elsewhere, the most illuminating and accurate way to delineate our experience of historical passage is by means of the two fundamental categories of destiny and freedom. By destiny I refer—as did Kierkegaard and Tillich—to what is given to us from the past into our present: not only the world with all its other persons, powers, realities, and forces, but also the self with all its own characteristics and powers—or lack of them. Freedom refers to the indubitable fact that while that given to us is unremovable and unavoidable, what we do with it in the present and for the future remains in part open and up to us. While we must accept, appropriate, affirm, and work with both our own given self, however paltry, and the world about us, however discouraging, nevertheless there are open alternatives. In part, we can and do actualize the self that is becoming through our own decisions and our action, and we can in part reshape the world of the next moment of passage. This experience of freedom to choose the self and reshape the world has in our culture been known and expressed by the middle classes; it is still a matter of faith rather than of experience for the oppressed.

Now, deeply implied in Christian experience and symbolism is the affirmation that creation is good and that the continual process of the world is under the divine providence. In terms of the ontological structure just suggested, that means that essentially or in possibility each moment is characterized by this union of destiny and freedom that constitutes temporal finitude. That is to say, in essence and so in possibility each moment, in what is given to us and in our own capacities, represents creative opportunities for self-actualization and for enriched experience. This is, I take it, the only genuine meaning the affirmation of the goodness of the creation as historical could have: namely, that all of us have a genuine, and not a sham chance for realizing our own innate capacities and actualizing our possibilities. The radical political implications, uncomfortable as they may be, of such a theological affirmation are obvious.

My main emphasis at the moment, however, is on Israel's experience of her own estrangement from this essential goodness, as well as, naturally, her experience of the estrangement of others. In her case this was an experience of estrangement in relation to the covenant and so to the explicit presence of Yahweh among them, an experience thematized in the symbols of the fall and of a fallen history. How, then, are we to understand in our own terms the Hebrew insight referred to earlier that each act of sin has objective consequences in the community?

In the whole biblical tradition, sin is regarded as an act of freedom, an inward, spiritual act, an estrangement of the inward, personal center of the self in its relation to God, to others, and to itself. Yet, in historical passage, what begins in inwardness does not remain there; our actions, gestated in inward freedom, have objective consequences in the world immediately to come. In actualizing our freedom in each moment we reshape what follows. Thus do we miscreate as well as create; we warp as well as reshape the resulting self and its resulting world. Inward sin, in other words, qualifies, distorts, even obscures and overlays the destiny given the next historical moment, the self and the world that are given there and are bequeathed to those who follow us. In personal life, this is evident: the self can through its successive decisions and its accumulating habits close off gradually and inexorably the creative possibilities for its own continuing future, for its "presents" to come. In social existence, this is even more objectively manifest. Human creativity helps to fashion or to reshape out of what is given to it the social, economic, and political institutions in which subsequent humans live and which therefore form the "given world" for others and for generations to come. It is an all-too-familiar experience how each generation inherits from its fathers and mothers a confused, warped world which it tends to detest and repudiate; and then thirty years later it finds itself— to its horror—bequeathing the same sort of mess, in different colors and shapes perhaps, to its own sons and daughters.

On an even deeper level, inward sin is objectively manifest in oppressive social forms. In the continuing institutional structures of an entire epoch or culture—of class, property, and privilege, of social rank and authority, of political power and rule, of sexual domination, in short, all the familiar forms of institutional injustice—is evidenced objectively the inward estrangement of men and women from one another. What is evidenced is the turn to the self and for the self against the other, and thus the drive to suppress and dominate the other, inward tendencies marvelously and horribly spread before us in the distorted, oppressive forms of these institutions. Sin does have its social consequences in community in the aggressive and imperial policies of each generation, and in the warped, oppressive, suffocating institutions of each culture's historical life. This is not merely primitive; it is also true.

I would suggest that this fact of social inheritance of the objective consequences of sin—what Walter Rauschenbusch perceptively called the Kingdom of Evil—points to a most important aspect of the human experience of a fallen history: the experience of being fated, of being subject to a blind and cruel fate, of an ineluctable power in historical passage that crushes and overwhelms our freedom and closes rather than opens new possibilities for the future. To enter life as a victim of oppressive, exploitative, unjust institutions, for example, slavery or segregation, is to experience the "given" in one's existence as void of possibility, as radically closed to the chance of creative self-actualization or creative reshaping of one's world. It is to be denied one's humanity, to be denied the good creation. As freedom in historical passage "falls" into estrangement and sin, so created or essential destiny, the goodness of creation and of temporality, "falls" into fate or threatens to become fate. Thus—and here is the important point—is excluded in the next moment for all those so fated the appearance of genuine, self-creative freedom, of real relations to others, of possibilities for the future, the goodness of being human. In this way, the inner reality of the bondage of our human freedom does not remain only inner. It is also manifest in the subsequent outward distortion of historical institutions, in part themselves the creatures of human creativity. Our inner self-concern results in a "given" for others that is characterized by the estrangement of fate. Social fatedness is thus neither arbitrary nor unintelligible in history; blind, uncaused, and inexplicable. Nor is it, as Marx thought, the *cause* of inner estrangement. Rather is it the inexorable *consequence* of estrangement. But fatedness, itself the effect of the sins of others, is the immediate source of untold suffering of the denial of the human, of the distortion of the possibilities of historical life, of the loss of a future and thus of hope. It is in the experience of being fated, of being a victim of historical sin and its consequences, as much as in that of being a perpetuator of sin, that evil is undergone, the goodness of life and its possibilities are obscured, and bitterness and despair emerge.

The historical situation of fatedness calls, therefore, dramatically— and here the Old Testament is also clear—for political liberation. This is not, let us note, a liberation from sin. But as we have shown, it is a liberation from the dire consequences of sin, from the fate which sin continually creates and recreates for others in and through objective social structures. Political action is directed against fate in this sense, against the continuation or the appearance in the future of a social and historical given that is crushing to self-actualization and to creative shaping of the world. Political action seeks to transform fate or the threat of fate into destiny, into an institutional given in our social world that remains open to new possibilities and to our own actualization of those possibilities. As is evident, such social action is a direct requirement of any life of faith and of obedience, and also of a theological understanding of history. For the warping of our social world, its fatedness for others, is the direct result of sin and the most immediate cause of the suffering of the children of God.

To change or reshape a political or economic order is not to eradicate sin: the democratic and egalitarian movements of the eighteenth century had effects but not that effect, as current American life shows! But such change will reduce the scope and the scourge of sin, and it will liberate sufferers from some of the consequences of sin. To take a current example: a cleansed South Africa will, we may be sure, still be characterized by widespread selfishness. But because of institutional changes lives will be freer, more secure, more dignified, more in control of their own futures. Real possibilities for a more authentic humanity, now closed by fate, will be there.

A second and related biblical theme about evil in history is what we may call the prophetic mistrust of power, the tipping of the balance in prophetic judgments against those who are mighty, or who are considered wise, good, righteous. This theme is also radically expressed in the weakness and suffering portrayed in the servant songs and in the Magnificat. As my preceding remarks have made clear, the problem of sin is universal, characteristic of the weak, the ignorant, the outcast as well as the strong and the established; fatedness does not, unfortunately, of itself necessarily result in an increase of virtue. We all, powerful and weak, female and male, actualize the given presented to us in warped and self-destructive ways. This inward estrangement in those who are weak, however, has little effect except on themselves and on their own; it barely touches the wider world of others. On the other hand, the inward estrangement of those who are mighty in any regard both affects others directly because of their power and also reshapes the given world of others. It is the mighty and the wise who are creative of and effective within the forms of social life and dominant in the continuance of those forms. And, as Marx noted, they shape those forms to serve their own interests. Consequently, it is the ruling classes that are primarily responsible for the distorted forms of social life, in both the latter's creativity and their distortion—rightly they tend to take credit for the first and rightly are they blamed for the second.

The conclusion of this discussion is that the powerful and the affluent are not more sinful than others—as some political theologies have intimated. They are, however, more responsible for the forms of fatedness that any epoch bequeaths to its weak and so more responsible for suffering. And they defend with all their power these forms of fatedness and the symbols justifying them that they have helped to create, that support their interests and that they as a class embody. Thus, political liberation from social forms of fatedness generally means liberation from the power and dominance of ruling groups. This seems obvious to everyone except ruling groups! Only thus can there be new possibilities for an oppressed world; only thus can the nemesis, the breakdown, and destruction so clearly foreseen by the prophets be averted for Israel and for ourselves alike. It is never easy nor comfortable, but it is salutary, for our affluent class and dominant nation to recognize this biblical bias against the affluent and the powerful. Let us note that while the religious foundations of any culture always tempt organized religion into a conservative, even oppressive role, into an alliance with the establishment, the demonic possibilities of any culture, as of any sacred tradition, correspondingly call for true religion to take a socially critical, a radical, possibly even a revolutionary role, into an alliance with the oppressed and the fated. Consequently, acts of political liberation almost always represent acts against the power and dominance of history's ruling elites—another important point for us in our powerful present to recall.

Both Scriptures emphasize the estrangement and fatedness of our common life, the inner bondage of our freedom, the outer bondage of our fatedness, and the judgment of God on these individual and social results of sin. Nevertheless, this is by no means their final word either about our inner personal life or about our historical social existence. For the major theme of both testaments is of the coming of new possibilities into human life, the freeing from the bondage of freedom and of fate—and, in the end, of death. This theme of the new covenant—a new relation to the law inside and a new social and historical reality outside, the messianic reign—is the central promise of the Old Testament. Its proclamation as having come is the central affirmation of the New Testament. In a short summation like this of the political dimensions of theology, I cannot emphasize or even clarify this entire gospel. And those aspects of the gospel relevant to inward, personal liberation, liberation from the inner bondage of our freedom, the redemption from sin and finally from death, aspects expressed in the Christological symbols or incarnation, atonement, and resurrection, and elaborated further in the themes of justification, sanctification, and the work of the Spirit have been sketched in the earlier chapters of this book.

What I do wish to emphasize here in these remarks on a theology of politics is that the promise of new possibilities in both Scriptures, and the important symbols expressive of that promise, have social and historical, and therefore political, ramifications—as did the creative and providential work of God, and as did our estrangement and the divine judgment on that estrangement. The later prophets, as we know, are replete with a sense of inexorable nemesis and doom for the warped communal existence of the Hebrew people. The social institutions and forms established through the old covenant will, say they, be undone, uncreated so to speak, and an almost primal chaos will result. But—and here sounds the unexpected, astounding, prophetic note—new possibilities are there in the future, new possibilities in the outward, communal structure of life as well as in its inward obedience.

Taking this central theme of the prophets again analogically in order to interpret general history and God's action within it, we can say that confidence in divine providence means confidence in the appearance of creative new possibilities in social life even in the hopelessness of an oppressive and unjust situation, or in the midst of the evident destruction of still-creative forms and structures given to us from the past. As Tillich said, it is confidence, despite a situation of manifest hopelessness, in the appearance of a new social kairos and the possibilities of liberation latent there. Creative political action must take place long before its fruits are empirically or historically visible. It thus requires confidence in the possibilities of the future even when they seem to be in fact impossibilities. Thus is every reform or revolutionary movement dependent on a philosophy or mythology of history. Such confidence is also essential in a time of the disintegration of older orders and the imminent threat of nemesis, when the temptations to panic and to destructive selfish action rise. The Old Testament hope for a new covenant is not just the promise of a new future characterized by religious inwardness, by the appearance of the Christ and the establishment of the church community (though it is also that), as the tradition has overwhelmingly interpreted it. As the Old Testament makes clear, it also represents a historical and social hope, a confidence in God's creative action in the political and economic orders of secular history. As the judgment of God signals clearly the imminent destruction of unjust and oppressive orders, so the promise of a new historical covenant signals the coming of new historical possibilities, of new forms of liberation from the fatedness of the present.

To sum up: the work of providence, God's activity in the outward scene of history and of social passage, has three moments crucial for a political theology: the creative activity of providence in the formation of social structures of communal life, the judgment of God upon the warped character of these historical gifts, and now the promise and the appearance of new possibilities, of new forms of social existence. The balancing presence in Christian faith of the themes of inward liberation, the themes of sin and grace, atonement and justification, does not remove or replace this promise of outward liberation. Rather that balancing presence reminds us that within the continuing work of providence and so within the appearance of new and less oppressive social orders, in the political conquest of particular forms of fatedness, the problem of sin continues, the need for repentance and grace will be constant, and so the promise of forgiveness remains fundamental for our ultimate hope.

Finally, this union of inner and outer, and of both as dependent on and fulfilled in the presence of God, is most clearly manifest in the central symbol of the New Testament promise, the Kingdom. I need not rehearse here the many ahistorical and nonsocial interpretations that symbol has received both in the tradition and in present exegesis. It seems not to matter whether a supernatural, otherworldly or a personal, existentialist interpretation wins the day; in either case the political relevance of the New Testament is dissolved. Nevertheless, if one traces, as I have sought to do, the fundamental intertwining of individual and social, of personal and historical, of inner and outer in the whole Scripture, through the symbols of creation, providence, fall, and the promise of redemption; and thus if one views the symbol of the Kingdom as representing the culmination, the eschatological culmination, of the covenant people in all the transformations that that crucial symbol underwent, then these ahistorical interpretations seem very questionable indeed. The Kingdom does express, to be sure, the reign of God in the hearts of men and women; it does signal the stark opposition of God's love and justice to the historical world; and it does refer as well to the final culmination of history and of persons in history in God's eternal reality far beyond the bounds of space and time.

Nevertheless, as its earthly analogue, a social kingdom, indicates, this symbol refers also to a redeemed social order and ultimately to a redeemed history as well as to redeemed individuals. For we have seen that there cannot be the one without the other. It is for this reason that the prophetic requirements that the covenant community, and with it all communities, be just, and the prophetic promise of a messianic community of justice, order, and peace, legitimately fill in the outer and structural content of the promised Kingdom. That Kingdom represents therefore the perfected social community that corresponds to the personal and individual perfection of the figure of Jesus, a perfection realized only in him. The symbol of the Kingdom thus functions in relation to ongoing historical and political life as the individual perfection of Jesus as the Christ functions in relation to the crises, despair, and fragmentary realizations of individual Christian existence. It establishes the ultimate norms, the bases for judgment and for policies in relation to political and communal action, much as the individual perfection of Jesus' life sets the ultimate norms for our own fragmentary good works. Both, the complete sanctification of our individual existence and that of communal existence, remain eschatological hopes; in both areas alike our experience is of fragmentary fulfillment at best, and in both we remain dependent in the end on the forgiveness and the promise of God for ultimate fulfillment. But as inner and outer, individual and social cannot be separated at any point in Christian understanding, so individual and social salvation cannot be separated. The Kingdom as a symbol of redeemed community underlines the final social, as well as the clearly personal and individual, character of God's purposes in historical time.

A satisfactory discussion of the political dimension of theology, or the social dimensions of the gospel, has only been initiated at best by these remarks. The implications of the religious dimension of community life for the priestly role of the church in society; the implications of estrangement and sin of community life for the prophetic role of the church in the world; the implications of the resurrection for the hopes of the church in the future; and the implications of the Kingdom for the constructive politics of the church—none of these have as yet been drawn. However, I hope my argument has been clear that when we look closely at the central symbolic content of our faith, and through the spectacles of that witness at the divine activity and purposes in history— as that symbolic content illumines for us that activity—we find an understanding of God, of human being, and of history that is social and political in form. From beginning to end, through covenant people, betrayal and sin, promise, new covenant to final Kingdom, the inner and the outer, the personal and the communal, the moral and the political are intricately but continuously intertwined. Throughout, the divine redemptive activity is directed not only against inward sin and individual death, but also against outward fate. Throughout, the divine purpose is not only to establish an inner piety but also a just, ordered, and creative outer world. Throughout, the divine gift of love involves not only renewed inward motives but also renewed relations between people in community. The symbols expressive of the creative, transforming power of God in historical time—creation, providence, redemption, love and final end—each weave individual and community together into a new fabric, a new world of the inner spirit expressed objectively in and through a community of justice, of reunion, and of love.

5

SCRIPTURE, HISTORY, AND THE QUEST FOR MEANING

My topic is the relation of Scripture and its understanding to the understanding of history, to the discernment in the sequences of history of meaning or the promise of meaning. This relation may seem an obvious one to this society; and, to be sure, it has been taken for granted in the long tradition of Hebrew and of Christian thought about history and its meaning. For most of us, it is here, in *this* volume, in these two testaments, that are contained the light that illumines the dark, terrifying mystery of historical existence and the grace that offers promise not only of understanding but of creative courage and hope. And yet we must recognize that this correlation of Scripture and of history appears to most of the world around us to be anachronistic, parochial, and bizarre, a kind of methodological version, so to say, of Lessing's "ugly ditch." If it seemed absurd to Lessing's age to derive a truth of universal scope from one historical event, surely it is equally backward in our own to interpret universal history on the basis of one text—and one text at that which represents a variety of epochs and cultural situations and is crammed with diverse materials and wildly divergent viewpoints.

Clearly, as Karl Barth would say, this queer claim for one text to manifest the universal can become intelligible only through the category of revelation: only the divine Word can leap that "ugly ditch" from the particular to the universal; only through the Word can one text bear this transcendent role in truth and in grace. That point being granted to Barth, however—and, speaking as a systematic theologian, I agree completely with him on it—it is, I think, nonetheless true that this correlation of one text, especially a religious text, with the interpretation and comprehension of history is not as bizarre and naive as modern culture tends to see it. To most of the modern consciousness, liberal or Marxist, history is not at all an impenetrable mystery. On the contrary, all one has to do is "to look at it" carefully and responsibly, "empirically and scientifically" as we would say, to see its structure and so to understand the principles of its sequences and changes. In such an endeavor, how can one text or one tradition be given a crucial role? And in such an obviously *secular* endeavor, comprised at best of economic, political, psychological, and especially sociological and historical learning, insight, and methodologies, how can a *religious* text be relevant or helpful, let alone decisive?

It is this viewpoint that I wish here to contest as a misunderstanding of the way, as humans, we are in history and the way, consequently, we understand history and find meaning in it. Texts, religious symbols, and participatory principles of interpretation, I shall argue, dominate and shape every approach to history and to life within it; this is a pattern pervasive in cultural and communal interpretations of history. And not only that, I shall seek to suggest that an understanding of history based on Scripture, on the two testaments, fits the contours of history as we experience it. This dual argument does not constitute a natural theology. Only in the brightest and happiest of epochs, and then only among the privileged classes, is a natural theology based on the character of history conceivable. Thus, my argument presupposes some transcendent principle of meaning, that is to say, it presupposes revelation, which no natural theology can establish or encompass. Nevertheless, it is an apologetical argument based on the compatibility or correlation of history as experienced and comprehended to history as interpreted in Scripture, a correlation basic, I believe, to Scripture's own understanding of itself and its historical world.

Let me begin this discussion with what will seem obvious about human being in time as we experience it. Humans, it has often been said, are both in and out of history, immersed in it and yet in part transcendent to it. Thus arise the two senses of the word *history;* as the sequence itself of novel and unpredictable events and as a report on or interpretation of that sequence. For it is evident that human existence is in and out of history in two related but distinct ways. First of all, our being in history is characterized by the polarity of destiny and freedom; of a given (destiny) from our own past and that of our world, a given which constitutes us, forms and shapes us, pushes us inexorably in a determined direction, and with which, whether we will or no, we must deal in all our actions. This unremovable destiny is balanced by the unavoidable requirement to decide and to act now in creative response to that given, within its limits but in the light of its possibilities (freedom). Thus is history characterized on the one hand by trends and continuities arising out of a given destiny, and on the other by contingency and novelty arising out of the unpredictability of human response, decision, and actions in the face of that given. The given was once itself undetermined, itself mere possibility; now it is there, shaped, unavoidable; what we do with it is limited by these conditions but never determined by them. Conditions, said Gordon Leff, become *history* only when they elicit a human response. History is destiny in union with freedom, neither one alone. We are in history as dependent on the conditions given from beyond ourselves; we are "out" of it as capable of responding in novel ways to those conditions. In history, actuality is balanced by possibility and destiny by freedom; and the union of the two makes historical events.

Secondly, while humans are *in* the stream of history, pushed by it in unwanted directions, threatened by its plethora of menacing forces, and lured by its unexpected possibilities, humans are also "out of it" in memory and anticipation. Spirit transcends history by surveying its past and, in that light, envisioning its possible future, by uniting, in other words, its destiny and its freedom, its unavoidable actualities from the past and its range of possibilities for the future. In each act of freedom in relation to destiny—in each personal and in each political act—remembered past and anticipated future are brought together first in comprehension and then in decision. Again, embeddedness in time and transcendence over it unite to make event. Thus does eternity, transcendent over time but a transcendence united with time, invade personal and communal life in historical understanding and in political actions alike. In any case, it is for this ontological reason, because of the character or structure of human being in time, that there is, for any historical understanding to be achieved or for any personal or political act to take place, the necessity of bringing what is remembered and interpreted and what is perhaps to come into a meaningful unity, a unity of understanding and of meaning—so that ongoing life, creative action towards the future, is possible. The deep involvement of human being and meaning *in* historical passage, *in* history, and yet its ability to survey and partially to direct that passage, create together the necessity of giving to the sequences of time a *logos,* a structure of order and meaning in terms of which both understanding and purposive action become possible. Political consciousness is requisite for political action, and for both a *theory* about the sequence of events is necessary.

Political action is both unavoidable and central in historical existence. It represents the centered action of a unified community through its "legitimate" leaders, in response to the given crises and opportunities of its common life. Since we all exist communally, political action is, therefore, the way human freedom expresses itself and is present communally, that is to say, in historical life. For history is constituted by the life and action of groups. And for a political act expressive of freedom, as for historical reflection itself, a unified understanding of the past, of the present, and thus of the possibilities of our future is necessary. Also involved or presupposed in creative political action is a firm grasp of the norms and of the potential meanings of life in time. In history and in communal life the practical and the theoretical tend to fuse into one—as the continuous role of savants or wise men in active political life illustrates. And both presuppose a vision of the structure and the meaning of the total sequence of events in which that community finds itself.

It is for these reasons, deeply embedded in our ontological structure as "finite freedom," as in yet out of history, that myths—symbolic visions of history as a whole—appear as basic to all important political speech, and that a general vision of history is presupposed in all historical understanding, even that which claims to be "scientific." Ingredient in these myths or visions of history—at least as they function communally—is some understanding of or theory about the ultimate sovereignty that rules history, its magisterial or ruling forces, be they evolutionary, economic, psychological, or theological; some view of an ultimate order in these sequences; some vision of an ultimate norm for communal life in history; and some sense of its ultimate meaning and thus of grounds for shared hope. Organized "religions" have traditionally provided that symbolic structure, orienting communal life in time to some permanent order and meaning. In a secular world, so-called ideologies, for example, liberal progressivism and Marxism, have done the same thing. Thus are politics and religion always interrelated in communal life. For it is the mythical vision (religious or secular) structuring this order and meaning of history that provides the basis for legitimate political rule, the guidelines for acceptable political action, the standards and goals for society's vocations, and the aims for its patterns of education. Every culture, as Paul Tillich reminded us, has such a "religious substance," an apprehension of ultimate being that structures our ultimate concerns, and that, as we have indicated, symbolically structures the ultimate and sacred horizon within which each community and each facet of its culture lives and becomes in time.

It is consequently no wonder that history, politics, and religion have always been so deeply intertwined. It is in the ongoing stream of historical process that communities face the crucial issues of their life and death, of security and insecurity, of freedom from fate or subservience to it, of the enhancement or the loss of meaningful existence—that is to say, that they face "religious" issues. And it is here in the sequences of temporal change that their freedom is most sorely tempted to actions of vast sin or self-destruction, or that they are called on for strength, courage, justice, and compassion. The issues of our being and of our nonbeing, our ultimate concerns, appear as much for communal life as for individual existence *within* historical sequence in dealing with an unavoidable given and in facing an unknown and often uncontrollable future.

Despite all their knowledge and their technology, modern men and women have not transcended this ontological structure of temporality and finitude, nor escaped the terrors and anxieties of history, the threats of fate and of non-being menacing their future, nor lost their need for confidence and hope in the open possibilities for that future. As much as older cultures, therefore, modern life has needed, and depends on, a "mythical" vision of history such as we have described. Thus is there a religious dimension in all cultural life and to all political speech and understanding, as much in contemporary as in ancient times. As a consequence, theological understanding—the understanding of the meaning of historical being in terms of some constellation of religious-type symbols—is always relevant to the comprehension of history. Or, to put it another way, any global understanding of history—again one thinks of liberalism or of Marxism—foundational for political and theoretical life alike, has a religious or a theological dimension or component. It includes a mythical structure providing for those who are committed to it an understanding of their own role in the global history of good and evil, an ultimate norm for cultural life, and a sense of meaning and of hope for the unknown future. To correlate *religious* documents structured by *religious* symbols with the interpretation of history is, therefore, by no means aberrant or merely traditional. Each modern secular ideology, however it may strain to be based on science or historical understanding alone, takes to itself religious elements whenever it functions as the common schema for the interpretation of a community's visual history.

Despite their necessity, such global visions of history are hard to come by and harder to verify. As every culture (except perhaps our own) has realized, the order and meaning of the structure of historical events is at best opaque, its key elusive; it represents a mystery with only dim and fragmentary facets of meaning. And it is certainly true that history presents us with an exceedingly complex and rich scene. As the story of collective human action in relation to natural and social changes and to unexpected historical events, history includes all the multifaceted dimensions, factors, and "causes" characteristic of individual human existence. To seek to understand it as if it were merely an aspect of changing nature characterized by invariant and determined physical relations alone, by so-called social laws, is thus a serious methodological error. Contingency and freedom are deeply ingredient in its structure, and so the possibility of real alternatives and the actuality of unexpected novelty continually upset any simple causal or rational order.

Three other factors add to this complexity and opaqueness of history.

(1) The curious observer of history, however objective he/she may seek to be, is herself involved in the history she observes, ultimately concerned with the direction of its current—for her life itself glides on them or sinks because of them. Thus is her vision shaped by her interests, and her interests by her location in the historical order. The fortunes or misfortunes of her class, sex, race, nation, epoch give form to her view and shape the optimistic or pessimistic mood that governs every such vision. For this reason myths about history, unless subjected radically to critique, are both partial and ideological; each is a limited perspective directed all too sharply by special interest as well as by particular insight.

(2) The sequences of history that are surveyed are always incomplete. The significance of each event, like election returns early on, is not yet "in," and so the meaning—even of a short span of events—is as yet neither settled nor evident. Consequently, visions of history are at best studied guesses, projected hypotheses, matters as much of communal

commitment and hope as of any precise verification or clear conceptual understanding. They are in fact "religious myths," held communally for existential as well as theoretical reasons, massively influencing life but limited in their universality and verifiability.

Any tomorrow can effect radical changes in the meaning of every piece of the data on which a vision of history is built. In a brief span of time, a novel sequence of important events can sink the most formidable and apparently permanent social or economic trend almost without a trace. Two examples come immediately to mind: predictions of a stable future for an agrarian society made in the Richmond or Montgomery of 1856 would have seemed bizarre indeed in 1875. And even Herman Kahn, who boasted that a "scientific futurology" could at last peer reliably into our probable future had, in his book on the year 2000 published in 1970, as yet no intimation at all of the ecology crisis, the crisis of world natural resources, that two short years later was to explode and qualify, if not falsify, every one of his graphs and expectations about our common world future. The past is itself not yet finished, and the future is radically unknown and unknowable. These ontological facts both elicit our *need* for a meaningful vision for this opaque passage in which we are, and yet they also prevent us both from being too clear about what we dimly see or from being too certain about the validity of our reports and our vision of things to come.

(3) History is alienated or estranged from its own structure. It seems never to be what it could or should be, what its possibilities either promise or require. Since this alienation arises in large part from our freedom, it includes our common responsibility. History, said Tillich, is estranged, and its estrangement is sin; or, as Augustine and Reinhold Niebuhr said, history is "fallen," and we are each alone and all together involved in that fall. As theory this sounds old-timey, moralistic, and even "small town" or naive. As historical experience, however, it is continually validated and revalidated. Glowing possibilities, both personal and social, do sour and become tasteless or demonic. Think of the waxing power of Europe in the seventeenth and eighteenth centuries, or that of America in the postwar world. And yet now the power of Europe is gone, and that of America declining—and each is for the forseeable future paying dearly for the exploitation, the oppression, and the conflicts which characterized the ways each actualized their own possibilities. The "given" which each older generation presents to its children, what they have done with their world, so full of possibilities in their

youth, festers, as they hand it on, with hidden or open sores that cause endless pain and can become lethal for the new generation that follows. My father's generation inherited from its parents the world of the First World War; mine, Hitler's world and with it the Second World War; and *think* what a mass of tangled corruption, of a world fraught with injustice, oppression, greed, and demonic possibilities our children will inherit from us! This corruption of history's ideal possibilities is the experienced actuality of history. This estrangement of actuality, to be sure, is clearer in some ages and to some groups than it is to others; but it is characteristic of all times and places. Yet it is also true that in the midst of this deep alienation characteristic of actuality, possibilities of the creative new do appear, hope and confidence are deeply felt, and unexpected healing is experienced.

Thus is there added to the complexity of history, and the involvement of every observer in it, a further dialectical complexity that requires a very subtle and rich—and also "religious"—set of categories. First there is the ontological-anthropological structure of history of destiny and freedom whereby each finite actuality is or can be given new possibilities for the future. Secondly, there is the experienced alienation whereby destiny becomes fate and freedom seems stripped of genuine possibilities. And, finally—a "fact" expressed in all religious visions—there appear redemptive forces of healing, of reconciliation, of reunion, and of new beginnings. Because of this dialectical complexity, secular theories of history become "ideologies" when they begin to function socially, that is, they all include finally a depiction of the career of good in the midst of evil, a story of redemption, however unintelligible or unempirical it may be, from the evil that obscures our historical present. And for this same reason, explicit religious visions of history are often more subtle and therefore more empirical (that is, closer to the facts of history) than are most purely cognitive "scientific" or philosophical visions. For each religious view tends to include some version of this religious dialectic established by alienation and redemption as well as the ontological limits and possibilities inherent in finitude and in freedom. No general interpretation of history can ignore the pervasive patterns of evil that engulf historical life, any more than it can ignore the possibilities implicit in freedom. Without a religious dialectic of alienation and redemption, however, such views misinterpret those patterns evident in historical life; they either emphasize the positive structure and harmony of passage and the possibilities of historical life (if the observer belongs to a fortunate group in a fortunate epoch) in an unwarranted and soon-to-be falsified optimism, or, concentrating so heavily on the actuality of evil, they speak only of fatedness, failing to discern the new possibilities and the forces for reconciliation latent in historical experience.

Biblical symbolism includes each of these levels of dialectical complexity, and that is perhaps the explanation for whatever persuasive theoretical power it may possess. In its symbols of creation and providence, and its consequent understanding of human existence as dependent finitude, and yet a free finitude directed to the ultimate and the sacred, that is, as creaturely and yet made in the Image of God, it presents a structural or ontological understanding of existence that clarifies and affirms the finitude and yet the self-transcendence characteristic of human life in time. With its further "religious" categories of estrangement and sin on the one hand and of revelation, redemption, and reconciliation on the other, it encompasses the second dialectic pervasive in existence I have just outlined.

It should be noted, however, that this illuminating complexity has led to two divergent and often clashing interpretations of biblical symbolism, that of natural theology and Pelagianism, and that of sin and grace. Seen from the perspective of this dialectical complexity, both of these antithetical traditions take their rightful place as, on the one hand, legitimate but, on the other, as partial. The first of them, conceived usually in an optimistic era, and from a privileged spot in which personal and historical possibilities seem plentiful, sees clearly history's fundamental ontological structure of creative destiny and of pervasive freedom for new possibilities. Thus, discerning an order and meaning to history's sequences, it concludes "rationally" that this evident goodness of life requires and so implies a divine power, a divine wisdom, and a divine bounty. When through the "good luck" of a fortunate epoch the ontological structure of history can be clearly seen, natural theologies, philosophical theisms, and an emphasis on human freedom abound and dominate theological reflection—but, understandably, such theologies, based on an apprehension of the obvious goodness and meaning of ordinary life, can only dimly discern the tragic elements of existence and so barely appreciate the full scope and meaning of the gospel.

In contrast, for other biographies, other classes, and other epochs, the alienation, the fatedness, and the suffering of history are deeply experienced. Destiny, with its promise, has seemed consistently to become a stifling fatedness to suffering and to meaninglessness, and the hope for new possibilities seems only an illusion. Freedom is aware only of its own bondage and its responsibility for that bondage. Sin, fate, and death appear to be the factors that alone rule actuality. In *that* sort of situation, the ontological structure of history as characterized by freedom and by novel, creative possibility disappears as do landmarks in a heavy fog at sea. And at that point, suave clerical assurances of the goodness, order, and possibilities of life and of a benevolent ruler of events seem to be a cruel jest if they are not an ideological sham, a turning away from obvious injustice in order to maintain and justify exploitative privilege. The longing for rescue from the anxiety, terror, and guilt of historical actuality replaces grateful celebration of its maker and serene confidence in divine justice. Understandably, now the more "religious" and less philosophical categories of sin and grace come to the fore as characterizing experienced actuality. Creation and providence, although still providing the ontological grounds for God's judgment and God's grace alike, seem ideologically suspect, a self-interested justification and blessing of an evil world. Here too, however, a theological error can appear if this emphasis is pushed too far. For the Gospel and the promises of grace make no sense unless the world is God's creation and under God's ultimate sovereignty. Both of these interpretations are, therefore, genuine intuitions of the character of historical existence, and both emphasize essential and crucial biblical symbols—and both consistently detest the vision of history and of the Christian religion that the other proffers! Possibly an awareness of the complexity and the opaqueness, even the mystery and depth, of historical process will help us to appreciate the dialectical richness and even the apparent paradoxes of our common biblical symbolism.

In any case, the main thrust of my argument is that both the character of human participation in history and the consequent complexity of history call for mythical and theological understanding. We cannot just "look at" history to uncover either the structure or the meaning of its sequences. Some deep assumed principle of interpretation is always at work whenever we think about temporal passage or seek to act within it. Such presupposed principles answer questions about the relation of determinism and freedom, about the meaning and scope of evil in time, about the possibilities available to life in time, about the redemptive forces available or not in history—in short, a global or mythical vision compounded of metaphysical, psychological, and religious elements. The history of religions provides us with explicitly religious variants of these global symbol systems; modern ideologies such as liberalism and

Marxism provide us with secular versions of the same. Each shapes and gives substance to a community's life by uniting that community through its vision of history and the role it gives that community in history. The religious substance of each creative culture is largely constituted by such a vision of history and of its meaning. Each is in turn quite particular; each arises out of a religious or a cultural tradition; each has crucial texts to which to appeal. Thus, not only religious symbols but also participation in a tradition, and attention if not adherence to the texts formative of that tradition, are constitutive elements of any communal interpretation of history. The logos of history is in each case borne by a given tradition and embodied in a given set of "scriptures," and both are crucial for communal and for political existence. History and interpretation, history and texts, are correlative. For historical beings, the universal is only available through the particularity of a given tradition and its texts, the meaning of history through a particular cultural or religious viewpoint. The role of scripture or its equivalent in human life in history, in shaping and unifying community, in guiding action and in comprehending the future with courage and hope, is no Christian or Jewish aberration destined to die out. It is essential to our human historicity.

Having discussed and defended the particular—in tradition, symbolic structure, and scriptural texts—as essential to the interpretation of past history and to action within present and future history, let me now turn directly to *our* particular case, to *our* Scriptures, and see how they serve to discern the meaning of events as we experience the latter. Are they illuminative of the structure and meaning of historical passage; and does this illumination provide a creative framework, inspiration, and guide for praxis? I think they do—though any arguments at this level are so circular in character as hardly to count as demonstrations.

As I have argued in chapter 4, in the Old Testament understanding of history there are three distinct moments or stages characterizing historical passage as Israel experienced that passage. First of all, there was the divine constitution or "creation" of the people as a people and of their cultural life in all its facets. There can be little question that for Israel, her cultural life had been constituted by Yahweh as probably the paradigmatic act *within* history of creation: it was God, not they, who established the covenant, who gave the sacred law covering all aspects of cultural life, and even who established the political institutions (the judges and later the kings) who governed them. And the main continuing role of Yahweh in relation to this people was the parental one of nurture, fostering, and protection, not so much of individual Hebrews but of the community as a community and the culture as a culture. Israel's culture was, if there ever was one, one explicitly with a "religious substance," one founded directly by God and one preserved and ruled by the divine actions in history. It is not inappropriate, therefore, to regard as "biblical" the viewpoint that each creative culture, insofar as it lives on a religious substance, is established in and through the presence of the divine, apprehended or received, to be sure, in different ways than this, but nonetheless grounded there.

The second moment, as we have noted, is the appearance of estrangement or alienation, of the "fallen" character of the life of even a chosen people. Specifically, this estrangement appears in Scripture as the betrayal of their covenant, a corruption of the gracious gifts received in and through the creative divine constitution of their communal life. This betrayal and corruption characterized the entire extent of Israel's experienced and recorded life within the covenant, whatever minimal "doctrine" of the fall they might have explicitly expressed. As they knew well and repeatedly experienced, the sins of the fathers *are* visited on their children's children. Thus, for them this alienation was one root, if not *the* root, of the tragic events and ultimately of the nemesis which increasingly threatened Israel's existence, as what we call the "prophetic interpretation" of their history makes clear. For she finally came to see this nemesis as God's judgment on her, a judgment so severe and total that it seemed (at least to Isaiah and Ezekiel) to betoken the *un*creation, the *un*raveling, and the *dis*integration of the creative culture Yahweh and this people had together raised up. It is surely no exaggeration to claim that this experience of betrayal, a betrayal of *our* creative covenant, and this threat of tearing down and even of approaching nemesis apply equally to our *own* experience, whether to the experience of Western culture generally or to that of our own American commonwealth.

The final moment is also prophetic, though it was, so to speak, "signaled" throughout the history by Yahweh's frequent and unexpected acts of repentent mercy. This is the promise of a new covenant beyond the destruction of the old, a new creative, redemptive act of Yahweh, the promise of new possibilities in historical life even though the old had now become corrupted, judged, and dismantled. The promise of such a new covenant—of new religious and cultural possibilities—was what provided, in the midst of the experience of social disintegration, hope for the future—though, let us recall, it was rarely welcomed by those presently in power. This theme too finds its echo in our modern experience: confidence in its validity provides the hope so often proclaimed in liberationist movements, and fear of the appearance of the radically new characterizes every established or First World power, capitalist and socialist alike.

These three moments characteristic of ongoing history as a whole have been drawn from the Hebrew Scriptures. They are, as a moment's thought will confirm, expanded, deepened, and refocused around one event or series of events in the New Testament, the life and destiny of Jesus, who is the Christ. There, divine constitution, divine judgment, and new creative act become incarnation, atonement, and resurrection/parousia, aspects of *history,* to be sure, but not of *ordinary* history. While this deepening and refocusing in the New Testament is central to any Christian interpretation of history, we have no time to develop its full implications here. Thus, I would in closing like to return to the three moments that delineate a biblical interpretation of the general structure of ongoing history and ask how they illumine for us the contours of our own historical experience. Certainly they are not, as we have seen, totally strange either to ordinary experience of history or even to ordinary views of history. In what, then, does their difference consist; and what does this difference or uniqueness add to our understanding of history and to our praxis within it? What we shall find, I think, is that on the one hand each of these three moments—divine constitution, divine judgment, and divine restitution or renewal—appears in its biblical form as apparently increasingly *incredible;* it is a truth about history and ourselves which is steadily harder to recognize, and, to be honest, which we don't *want* to recognize. Still, on the other hand, we shall see that a closer and more careful look at the real situation shows each to be increasingly validated by that real situation.

Every creative movement or epoch in history believes in divine constitution. They may not put it that way, but intrinsic to any communal myth or vision of history is the deep belief that now at last the essential purpose and goal of history has manifested itself embodied in historical community—and, needless to say, in *our* community. It is as if the ultimate grain of history has at last revealed itself in us; the center and goal towards which events had been moving and the pattern which will set the form of subsequent historical life are now plain and embodied in our communal life. So Christian nations and empires interpreted themselves in contrast to their pagan, infidel, or heretical contemporaries. So had China and Japan alike understood their role or destiny; and, ironically, despite their deliberate repudiation of the category of the sacred, so did the Enlightenment and its two children interpret themselves: liberal/democratic culture (this *was* the theory of progress) and now most recently Marxism. What distinguished the biblical (and possibly the Chinese) account from those others is that the divine is not regarded as indissolubly bound to the culture in question, as intrinsic to it, however creative it may have been. Rather in the scriptural view the divine constitution eventuates in a convenantal relation in which betrayal and even abrogation are possible, and in turn which can result in judgment and ultimate repudiation. In other words, the divine creative act has become characterized by a moral relation in which the issue of the justice of the community is crucial to the relation of the divine and its constituting power to that community. As a new and unexpected dimension of historical life, the norm of justice has become central to history, and with it the conceivability and the possibility of communal self-criticism at the deepest level appear.

Likewise, every culture has the experience of and belief in estrangement, alienation, and guilt. To all cultures, evil is well-nigh pervasive, human life by and large wrongly lived, immorality generally rife, and whatever good there may be vastly precarious and even endangered. To be sure, they manifest widely differing interpretations of these aspects of historical life and of what makes up good and evil; and each culture locates good and evil in vastly different places. To most cultures, evil lies in those who are deviant from the community and its ethos; and especially it lies in whatever forces are opposed to the community, in other words "our enemies." There among the "bad guys," deliberate wrongs are visible, malice and self-interest obviously rule, and thus the presence of real guilt is undeniable. Modern theory, social-scientific or Marxist, tends to deny guilt as a false category, itself expressive only of sociological or psychological alienation. Modern politics, on the other hand, domestic or international, is as replete with it and with the moral judgments that lie back of it as was that of any epoch.

Again, what is unique about the biblical interpretation of this aspect of history is that the pervasiveness of evil, of moral wrong, of guilt, is made universal or all-inclusive. Thus, and here surely is the crucial point, it includes *us* as well as the enemy, the good guys as well as the bad. Clearly, the possibility of a new sort of communal self-understanding is appearing here, and a new sort of transcendence, a self-understanding that can be self-critical and still affirm its own destiny, and a transcendence that yet remains constitutive of the creative value and the potential moral health of the historical community. The biblical interpretation is becoming increasingly strange and incredible to ordinary wisdom, and yet—as we promised—more and more in tune with the actual contours of concrete historical experience.

In a sense, hope is universal, at least wherever a culture or a community is on the rise, feels itself to be gaining strength, and thus finds itself facing a brightening future. However, despair, hopelessness are also in the same sense universal. For the historical forces that impel a movement forward can also, and frequently do, desert it or turn against it; or, as we have noted, a cultural community may well bring about its own nemesis. Confidence in liberalism and Marxism alike have waned for our immediate generations. Each in its own way seems to many of its adherents spent as a historical force, its glowing possibilities corrupted into sordid actuality, and its theories contradicted by too many historical facts. In such a situation, promise, hope for the future, requisite for creative political action, seem impossible; and as a consequence, forces representing only the past or representing only sheer power move to the center of the stage. To believe in new possibilities in the midst of an apparently desperate situation, a situation with no possibilities, is therefore almost impossible; existentially, the promise of a new covenant can be quite incredible. Such belief depends not only on a confidence in the sovereign forces of history; it also requires a mode of transcendence in the object of faith of which few visions of history are capable. Such a situation of despair about the future seemed itself incredible short decades ago; but such may well become our situation in the near future.

The uniqueness of biblical hope, however, is not only that it promises new possibilities in even the darkest hours. It is also that what we can genuinely and certainly hope for is not necessarily what we expect or even count on. It is a genuinely new possibility, upsetting and even contradicting what *we* are as well as what our opponents are, against *us* as good Democrats as well as against them as bad Republicans or Communists! Again, transcendence has creatively entered the scene and made all the difference. But because the divine remains constant, it is a new convenant in continuity with the old that we have experienced and loved, and thus a valid object of our hope for the future. The cultural epoch that follows the demise of ours will not represent what either Washington or Moscow or Peking want; of that we may be certain. But because it is the *same* Lord who rules the future and its possibilities, that promise of the unknown may be faced with confidence and with hope. And this, I suspect, is at the moment both the most incredible and the most important of all the biblical words about history to us.

The SACRED
in a SCIENTIFIC
CULTURE

6

THE CREATIVITY AND AMBIGUITY OF SCIENCE

Our topic, which is more provocative than I might wish, stresses the ambiguity of science: its possibility, not unlike that of morality and religion, to be, strangely, an instrument of evil as well as a bearer of good. The reason is that science is not only a neutral and harmless method of inquiry and a consequent body of tested hypotheses, it is also a historical force of overwhelming creative power and significance, shaping the social existence of humankind in ever-new directions and transforming not only the character of the lives of men and women but also their understanding of themelves, of the history of which they are a part, their view of their destiny. And it also has, strangely and unexpectedly, an ambiguous career in modern life not unlike that of religion in former times. Our question, then, concerns the ambiguity of the role of science in our common social present and especially our future.

The creative—and I would like to emphasize the word *creative*—effects of science are spread before us in every aspect of modern social existence. It is through science that technology—which is itself as old as Homo faber—has developed to its present astounding levels; and it is through that technological development that industrialism has transformed every facet of our lives, personal and social. This interrelation of science and technology, while debatable on a theoretical level, is confirmed in the historical development of each: they have risen and fallen together in history, and continue to do so. Few funds for pure science are granted without an eye to practical application, as every lobbyist in

75

Washington knows. And no discovery in the most esoteric branches of pure science is announced to the public without specification of the potential "revolutionary practical uses" of the discovery.

Above all, as Francis Bacon said, empirical knowledge, knowledge of the forces that surround us in our world, means the power to control and manipulate those forces for human well-being. It means technological control over the mysterious forces and principles of life. Greater knowledge always means greater power. Thus, whether this be their intention or not, the "knowers" in any society bequeath to their culture ever-new powers to transform its life. It is for this reason that knowers, religious or scientific, are valued as well as revered by their society, the priest's robes and the scientist's white coat signifying much the same social role of the knower of significant secrets and so the doer of all-important deeds.

The creative effects of science on modern culture have been, however, by no means purely materialistic, the results of technology and industrialism on our material standards of living and thus on our health, comfort, and general security or well-being—great as these latter are. For in my view, science has been the most important formative factor in creating what we may call the modern *Geist*. By the modern *Geist* or spirit, I refer to that view of man and woman, of their world, of their possibilities, history, and destiny which has distinguished—as have also technology, industrialism, and their effects—modern culture from other cultures. A most crucial attribute of modern science has been its capacity to know what has not been known before, to be therefore creative of new knowledge, of new understanding, of new concepts, new views. A culture dominated by scientific knowledge has, therefore, developed a critical relation to tradition, even its own tradition, and a tolerance of the unaccustomed, the unorthodox, the deviant that is itself something new in history and for many of us who are not part of the scientific community a most precious aspect of modern culture owed largely to science. But new ideas mean, as we noted, new possibilities for life, new forms of life, a new and remade world, a new future. Thus, again out of science has come a new understanding of human possibilities, of the capacity of man and woman to reappraise and remake their world, and of history as the locus of these novel possibilities. From this has arisen a new understanding of man and woman as capable of controlling natural forces for their own use, of remaking their social and historical worlds, and thus of history as a realm of promise. If people in former ages felt themselves to be the victims of forces which they could neither understand nor control, through scientific understanding and technological control man and woman have come to feel themselves the masters of these forces and thus even of their own destiny. Science has given to human beings a consciousness of their own freedom in nature and in history unknown before, and out of this new self-awareness has come the buoyancy and the hope for the future characteristic of modern culture wherever it has penetrated.

Moreover, science has represented in our culture a most precious human attribute, the love or eros for the truth and the intrinsic joy, not to say ecstasy, to be experienced in relation to truth. Thus, it has provided our culture with much of its spiritual grandeur and given opportunity for countless persons to fulfill their lives in selfless commitment to the truth and to it alone. Science has, I believe, shaped the most significant and enduring form or model of human authenticity, of human excellence, that has been produced in our time. As a cultural force, therefore, it has been as creative in the area of our spiritual existence as in that of our material existence.

Few things in human life, however, are creative in moderation, or—even more important—are moderate about their own creative powers. Because it brought a quite new and more reliable sense of certainty in the knowing process, a new freedom from tradition and from absolute spiritual authorities, and a new confidence in the power of our freedom to control our future, science appeared to much of our recent civilization—to laymen, educators, philosophers, and scientists alike—as *the* salvific force in history. If only, said John Dewey, we could apply the scientific method and spirit to all our problems, those problems will recede; science will save us if only we harken to her. It was the two roles of science we noted that gave the new method of science this apparent saving power: as the bearer of testable and therefore valid knowledge and as the key to control. As with all saving religions—and science has been a religious force for our culture as Marxism has been for another culture—sacred knowledge establishes and guarantees the power to control whatever menaces us. Through that sacred knowledge, there is given to those who bear it—be they yogis, priests, or scientists—mastery over the fates and the key to future well-being. In the case of medieval religion, the sacrality of knowledge came from its divine source in revelation and from its power to save us from sin and death. In the case of science, it came from the objectivity of its method, the sharability of its conclusions, and its utility in technological application to the pressing problems of everyday life.

Whenever knowledge and control have such a sacral character—that is, whenever they promise salvation from what we take to be our most fundamental ills—they dominate the culture that forms itself around them. As religion had dominated the civilization of the medieval period, so science has dominated ours. It has determined or shaped education, molded our sense of human excellence, grounded our hopes for the future, and established itself as the queen of all the other disciplines of learning. It became quickly *the* method of inquiry according to which all the other *Wissenschaften* must remake themselves or be excluded from the academic court, a view reflected in many disciplines not recognized as "scientific" themselves. Its empirical and objective techniques represented to great numbers of people, scientists and nonscientists alike, *the* form of knowledge to which every other mode of knowing had to conform or be banned from serious consideration. Increasingly, to our cultural life (though not to many scientists) it alone defined what was real and effective in intelligible and rational experience. As logical positivism, the philosophical counselor, advocate, and handmaiden of the new queen, said: existential statements, statements of "what is the case in the world," are scientific in form, or else they are meaningless. Relevant reality is known and dealt with only in this way; all deviant claimants to knowledge, be they aesthetic, moral, philosophical, or religious, are merely emotive and so tell us nothing of what is real. The other disciplines quickly fell in line with the new queen; psychology and the study of humankind, social and political theory, literary criticism, history, philosophy, and, heaven help us, even theology sought to become "scientific" if they were to be recognized at all in academia—as in the medieval period every discipline claimed to have a theological foundation as the guarantee of its validity and of its usefulness to human welfare. And, as with all queens, there were rewards. As the church ended its reign owning one-third of Europe, so science in the modern university receives and uses the vast majority of private and public funds. Sacral knowledge and the power it gives over all that seems to threaten us makes of any discipline a queen. And let us note, just as it was not alone the theologians who made theology the queen but people of all sorts who revered as sacred and as saving the knowledge formulated in theology, so it was not alone scientists or even their spokesmen who brought science to this position of dominance but those in all walks of life who found scientific method to be the key to valid knowledge in all fields and to contain the cherished promise of greater human well-being.

Queens, however, are not always so; they have their day and then decline, possibly into banishment. Coups d'etat, palace revolts, and changes of rule take place in cultural as in political life. The development of modern culture since the Reformation and the Enlightenment has seen not only the rise of science to cultural dominance; it has also witnessed the decline of the church as foundational to social existence in all its aspects, and, correspondingly, the eclipse of theological understanding as the ground of every valid field of inquiry and so sovereign over all. As everyone familiar with this history knows, there were innumerable causes of this loss of ecclesiastical and theological sovereignty.

Central among them, I believe, was the fact that the church and its truth claimed an absoluteness that nothing human could or should claim. To be sure, the God to which Christian faith witnesses and the divine grace it proclaims are, I believe, absolute. But the human response to God, the historical forms of Christianity, its doctrines, its moral laws, its human institutions and clerical authorities—these were not at all as absolute, unambiguous, and "pure" as their representatives, in their enthusiasm for the saving power of religion, believed. Thus, the claim to absoluteness led in the end only to disaster for religion and for the society in which it was central.

Now, the main point of these remarks is that in our day we may well be, I think, witnessing a similar process: the gradual dethronement of the most recent queen. One could cite many evidences of this shift in cultural sensibility. The rise of the interest in the occult and in mysticism, so astounding among our educated youth, represents a direct challenge to the supremacy of the scientific consciousness and the world view it has created. And the general disillusionment with technology bespeaks a deep questioning of applied science as the answer to human problems. Any visitor to meetings of the National Science Foundation can feel there—even in that center of social prestige, economic power, and political clout—a new nervousness and uncertainty about the role of science, about, in fact, its predominance, in our cultural life.

If one seeks for the deeper causes of this widespread uneasiness about science, they lie, I believe, in the same profound "fault" as was evidenced in the career of the erstwhile queen, religion. There we saw that religion "fell" from sovereignty because, although it is an essential and very creative aspect of human existence, it made itself absolute, predominant over the other aspects of life, and the sole source of knowledge and of healing. I believe the same has been true of science, which is also, let me repeat, essential to life and a creative power of human being; and precisely because of that creativity has it been tempted to its fall. I shall seek to show this, and its ambiguous consequences, in relation to three important aspects of science as a cultural force.

There is, first of all, the question of the absoluteness of the scientific consciousness as the entrance into what is actual. Is the method of science the *sole* cognitive avenue to the real? Or, put in terms of our court analogy, should science—or any other discipline—be the ruling queen? Although a great deal of valuable philosophical thought has been given to this question since the rise of science—one thinks in our time of Husserl, Whitehead, Buber, and Tillich—I shall argue my point in terms of the career of science itself.

As we have seen, science has represented in our cultural life an intense and continuing experience of human self-transcendence: of the power of human inwardness and autonomy to rise above all prior conditioning to know the truth "objectively," of the power of inward commitment to the truth to transcend tradition and authority in order to achieve new concepts, and of the power of informed intelligence creatively to remake its world. The sense of the self as free, potentially "objective," and thus creative within the stream of events has been uniquely characteristic of our culture, of Enlightenment culture. It is, I believe, the direct result of science, or, better, of the experience of *being a scientist* within the scientific community. Modern man and woman have known of their own potential freedom over their own prejudices, their own baser desires, over tradition and conditioning, and over their world largely through the experience of themselves as knowers and manipulators which the members of the scientific community have for several generations enjoyed.

Here, however, a strange contradiction enters that is most significant. For scientific method knows only an *object,* never a self-transcending, free, committed, and creative *subject.* When science through its method speaks "officially" of human being, it can find no shred of evidence of such a creative, autonomous self. It finds only a complex, natural organism conditioned in all it does by the various factors: genetic, physical, chemical, biological, psychological, and social, which have made it what it is and which, for objective inquiry, determine its subsequent career.

On the other hand, however, the reality and effectiveness of human creative autonomy, of human subjectivity, have been vividly experienced, and in so far *known,* by the scientific community and through them indelibly impressed on human history. Yet that community, when it knows by the method that gave it this experienced and known freedom, knows and can know no such autonomy. Clearly, what this strange contradiction within science as a historical force signifies is that the reality which is experienced and known by the scientific community itself in doing science is much wider than the "reality" which the objectifying net of the scientific method itself can capture. This wider reality of the self, presupposed in science as a human activity, is known by the self-awareness of the scientist; not by objective inquiry, but in the practice of that inquiry, through the scientist's inner consciousness of himself or herself as the subject of the knowing process. Science *knows* the mysterious depths and freedom of the subject through the self-experience of the scientist. And it is this self-awareness of the scientist as a committed, transcendent, free, intentional, and creative self that has given the sense of subjectivity, autonomy, and freedom to our recent cultural life. Clearly, science knows much more than it officially says it knows. This contradiction reveals the error of regarding this method as the one or exclusive entrance into reality and truth; it shows how one-sided, and, in fact, untrue to its own deeper knowledge, a culture dominated exclusively by scientific method can be; and it helps to explain the deep and even angry reaction against an absolutized science presently so characteristic of our cultural life.

Secondly, an absolutized scientific method misunderstands the *object* of inquiry, that which the scientist seeks to know, insofar as what he or she knows through scientific inquiry is taken to represent the full reality of the object known. What cannot be known at all is not *there* for us; we use the word *knowledge* to specify what is taken to be real, independent, dependable, and in that sense "objective." To confine knowledge to one method, and to a method that abstracts away from all subjectivity, centeredness and uniqueness, is infinitely to constrict the world that is real to us in its depth and mystery; it is to objectify into a determined, subjectless realm all that with which we have to do. With men and women this is obviously a dangerous error, as if all others than the inquirers themselves were mere conditioned objects, empty spaces, as Tillich once put it, through which external forces pass. Such a view of human reality, expanded into the social and political arenas, would strip society of persons and create a social world of usable objects. The contradiction of this view of human being with science itself as a creative human activity, as with the rest of life, has already been pointed out.

Such a view of the object of knowledge, however, also has devastating consequences for our relation with nature, as we are fast discovering. The relation of scientific method to the technological and industrial use, misuse, and ultimate despoliation of nature is not merely that technology applies for the purposes of manipulation the knowledge gained by scientific inquiry. It is also an essential relation consequent on the objectifying character of inquiry itself. For scientific inquiry knows by manipulating its object, by converting its qualitative traits into homogeneous and therefore universal units, by investigating it with regard to its invariant relations with all that conditions it. Thus does inquiry strip its object of all its qualitative characteristics, its inherent integrity, unity, and centeredness. Such a world is known only through our manipulation of it; consequently, such a world has reality for us only insofar as it can be used by us for our own purposes. Objective inquiry, taken as our *sole* cognitive relation to reality, becomes the ideology of technological and industrial manipulation. In order to live creatively within nature, as well as with each other, we must allow ourselves to know the objects we encounter through participation and union as well as through objectification and manipulation. Again a mode of knowing creative as one aspect of our encounter with reality becomes destructive of nature and of ourselves if it is made absolute.

Thirdly, as we noted, perhaps the major component of the reverence for science in modern culture has been the promise which applied science seemed to offer for human security and well-being. Our culture has swallowed Francis Bacon whole: empirical knowledge, we have believed, is power to control the forces that run our world, the forces of nature, our genetic and psychological structures, and the forms of our society. Through such knowledge and the control it brings we can make our life infinitely better. History, however, has rudely wakened us from this Enlightenment dream. For control of the earth through technology has meant the misuse, pollution, and despoliation of the earth. Further, it has unleashed an infinity of industrial expansion and appropriation that threatens soon to divest the earth of its available resources. Thus, far from guaranteeing human survival and well-being, the expansion of our own technological control now precisely threatens that very survival and well-being. Ironically, that cultural force which once promised to free us in the future from all that menaced us—disease, hunger, cold, poverty, and irrational tyranny—to free us from the Fates, now is disclosed as itself a menacing and even mortal fate. History, and our own wills which help to shape history, now appear as much more mysterious, even demonic, than they once did.

The current despair about the scientific future to which I here refer bespeaks a vast change of cultural consciousness, a realization of the essential ambiguity of applied science which is quite new in our post-Enlightenment world. Homo faber has been regarded by us as the creature who through his practical intelligence was of all earth's creatures most capable of adaptability. Equipped with modern technology, this same Homo faber thus seemed the very paradigm of survival and of increased well-being. It now appears that Homo faber can, through that same power of practical intelligence, destroy both his world and himself with it. Does this mean that technological freedom, the power to shape and control events by intelligence, is the key to our extinction in history—our "fatal flaw"—and not to survival, as we thought? That would indeed be an ironic end to a culture that gloried in that freedom! It seems it may be—unless man is *more* than technological man and learns, not more about how to control nature, but more about the control of himself.

The absolutization of applied science as the cure of our problems, as the key to freedom from fate, has proved to be a mortally dangerous error. As the Greek and the Christian traditions have emphasized, more than technical knowledge is necessary for life; in fact techne by itself, as our ecological crisis shows, is inherently self-destructive. Knowledge and control of the self, of its limits, of the infinity of its concupiscence, of its inherent waywardness and capacity for self-destruction, is also necessary lest increased technical power spell disaster. Here, I believe, is the deepest reason for the fall of the queen: the salvation that she promised in the period of her pride has turned out to be lethal.

Clearly, modern scientific culture had placed the problem of human existence at the wrong point. It had seen the major problems of life to stem from our lack of control over the forces that impinge upon us from the outside; thus, it reasonably concluded that increased control over those forces would create an existence free of massive suffering and want. It forgot the mystery and ambiguity of the controlling self, of the *users* of science and technology, whose greater powers through knowledge may free them from external forces, but who remain bound by their own greed and insecurity to misuse those powers and so in the end to destroy themselves. It is the bondage of our will, not our ignorance or lack of power, that threatens our historical existence as a race. That science and technology could not by themselves cope with this more intractable problem, is no fault of theirs; neither one is equipped to do so. But that in their day of glory many of their enthusiastic spokesmen taught us to ignore these deeper issues and even to laugh them out of court *is* their fault. Again it was in the absolutization of scientific techne as a saving force in history that the error lay.

The fault, let me reiterate, lies not with science as intelligent inquiry, nor with technology as the application of knowledge, and certainly not exclusively with their representatives, scientists and technologists. These are in themselves good, evidences of the vast creativity of human existence, and replete with immense potentialities for human good. Incidentally, even though they may now threaten our survival, they are also paradoxically utterly necessary for that survival. We cannot now do without them even if foolishly we would. What has been our fault as a culture is not our knowledge but our pride in our knowledge, not our technical power but our misuse of that power in the service of our material insecurity, our national pride, our insatiable greed. To put it theologically, it is our common sin, not our knowledge, that now threatens us—just as before it was sin, not ignorance, that caused the most destructive of the earlier problems of our race. Like everything else that is human, including religion, science and technology can be, and have been, misused. To say this is to defend them from their fanatical detractors. But, let us note, to say this is also to admit that they are not omnicompetent, unambiguous saving forces in history. Other ways of resolving other types of problems, other forms of knowing, other disciplines are *also* necessary in human existence, necessary precisely if science and technology are not to destroy us. The queen can save herself from banishment only if—as religion had to do—she is willing to abdicate her role as queen.

What is called for, therefore, is a reassessment of science in our cultural life, and one conducted soberly by the scientific community itself and not alone by those on the outside who now tend to distrust it. Such a reassessment is always painful, as it surely was for religion when it came under vigorous criticism in the Enlightenment and post-Enlightenment worlds. It was hard for those deeply concerned with religion and conscious of its saving power in themselves to face the fact that sincere piety could as a cultural force be a repressive rather than a freeing factor and destructive rather than creative in social life. So it is now difficult for much of the scientific community and its lay adherents to give up the belief that scientific inquiry represents the one "pure," disinterested, and objective form of knowing, and the consequent faith that the application of organized intelligence to life's problem is likewise pure, disinterested, and unambiguous.

In a similar situation, the only way religion has been able to recover its own integrity and rediscover a creative role has been to take herself through such a painful process of reassessment, yes, even of repentance and disavowal. When others reassessed the role of religion, she found herself banished from the court. When the religious community itself asked the question: if religion be neither the spiritual authority governing all of public life nor the queen of all the disciplines, what *is* her role and status? Then a creative or at least tolerable answer appeared. Such is, it seems to me, one of the tasks of the scientific community as it faces what is surely to be a quite new future.

Although this reassessment is primarily a task for the scientific community, perhaps a friendly observer may make three suggestions. First, one of the "myths" of an absolutized science was that its knowledge, that is, the forms of its concepts and symbols, was purely self-generated, arising solely from scientific experience and scientific logic and thus in no way relative to the general notions circulating in its wider cultural environment.

Recent studies in the history of science, however, have shown that this understanding of itself as essentially independent of other aspects of culture was in great part an illusion. The categories, models, and paradigms of scientific understanding, at each stage of its development, have been related to and in many cases directly dependent on notions generated in other fields. As a human and cultural activity, science is *relative* to its historical context, expressing through its own specialized categories many of the economic, political, social, psychological, philosophical, and even religious presuppositions that have determined that environment—as, of course, does any formulation of religion. It does not, therefore, represent a "pure" or totally objective form of knowing validly dominant over all the relativities and partialities of culture in its other aspects. At each stage of its life, science itself represents an aspect of that same relative cultural vision, itself therefore to be corrected and supplemented by other aspects of culture and even by other cultures—and not only by its own future developments.

It is well known that no form of "orthodoxy"—orthodox Catholicism and Marxism have been good examples—understands its own doctrines through a careful study of the *history* of their development. On the contrary, each one on principle understands its own history only in terms of its present and absolute doctrines. It is not insignificant in this respect that science is not taught to young scientists in terms of its history as well as in terms of its present levels of development. In the vast majority of cases, science is studied and viewed by young scientists *only* in terms of its present point of development, as if controlled experiment and logic provided its only components, and the cultural matrices out of which scientific concepts arose historically were irrelevant to their full understanding. One suggestion, therefore, in the reassessment of science is that it be studied historically as well as systematically—as are art, social theory, literature, philosophy, and religion—and with the express aim, as in those other disciplines, of showing the intrinsic relation of its major models and paradigms to their changing cultural contexts. As religious orthodoxy has found, a historical account of any discipline is an effective detergent of the absolutization of that discipline's content and methods. A historical view of science will help in the achievement of a realistic reassessment of its actual status and role in cultural life.

Secondly, as I have argued, scientific inquiry does not represent the sole cognitive relation that men and women possess with what is actual. As Whitehead argued, like the sensory experience on which it is based, scientific method abstracts for certain purposes from the totally encountered world, from our constitutive relations with things, from awareness of the subject of knowing, awareness of natural beings around us, and awareness of persons as persons. To confine knowing to this one significant but objectifying method is to strip natural objects of their inherent reality and value, and persons of their selfhood, their creative freedom, and their humanity. Science must, therefore, see itself as only one aspect—to be sure, a most important and valuable aspect—of human cognitive creativity, and thus one supplemented by and dependent upon other aspects, if it is to take its rightful and not dominating role in our cultural life. Such a reassessment implies an acquaintance with other modes of cognition: in literature, in social existence, in the arts, in philosophy, and in religion. And it necessitates an understanding of the interrelations of these modes of knowing to science that only the philosophy of science and philosophical epistemology can bring. When theology lost its absolute base in revealed dogma, it was incumbent upon it to reinterpret religious knowledge in relation to the other valid modes of knowledge in culture, to history, to science, to psychology. Thus did the discipline of philosophy of religion come to prominence; and such a critical and philosophical interpretation of religious knowledge is now a part of all advanced education in religion, as is a study of religion's history. A corresponding reassessment of scientific knowledge in relation to the other cultural modes of encountering, knowing, and shaping reality would set science among the humane arts and thus help to humanize rather than to dehumanize our common world.

Finally, as we have seen, the application of scientific knowledge has revealed itself to be an instrument of human will and thus subject to all the distortions of which that will is capable. Knowledge is power, and power can corrupt, even when that power springs from knowledge gained through objective inquiry. Informed intelligence can be the servant of our greed and our desire for security; it has not, as was hoped, been their master. Apparently, the more technical know-how we possess, the freer we are to ravish the earth and to plunge ourselves into a new unfreedom of scarcity, conflict, and ultimate authoritarian control. The increase of humanity's power through applied knowledge has increased neither our virtue nor our wisdom. Rather by threatening our human well-being, if not our survival, that increase has raised the question of our virtue and our wisdom more sharply than ever. A scientific and technological culture has not made the existential and moral questions of religion irrelevant, as it had thought. It has posed those questions anew, and in a terrifyingly intense form, crucial to the realization of that culture's own potentialities and to the avoidance of that culture's own self-destruction.

Unfortunately, as Socrates and Saint Paul both knew, there is no available educational program—even a graduate or professional one!—that can guarantee either wisdom or virtue to any of us. Possibly, as in current religious studies, an acquaintance with the sociology of science—how ideological, class, national, and professional prejudices affect the formulations and even the application of scientific knowledge to the world's problems—and a study of the ethics of science will help a little. Together, the sociology and ethics of science can, if taken seriously as a part of the education of the scientist, open the eyes of the future scientific community to the dangers of their own increasing power, to the responsibilities of their own increasing power, and to their intellectual and moral dependence on legal, moral, and religious wisdom if they are to be creative and not destructive in our common future. In the end, however, science and applied science—like every other aspect of human creativity—must learn to live with and to deal with the vast ambiguity of precisely their own creativity—and that is an existential, moral, and religious problem facing every profession, but new, I suspect, to the scientist, as it once was new to the priest. For the lesson of history, and now of the history of a scientific culture—and surely also the message of the gospel—is that it is the very creativity of men and women that can spell their doom, that their knowledge can be turned into blindness, and their power into self-destruction. To recognize this mystery latent within even that which is most creative in our life is a part of wisdom and the beginning of repentance. Such repentance on the part of all of us who have helped to create the very dubious destiny we shall bequeath to our children will possibly help to soften that destiny. Without such repentance and such new humility by all of us in a scientific and technological culture, the future that science brings to us— as well as the future of science itself—may well be darkness and not light.

Such wisdom and repentance may also become an entrance into a much deeper faith. As we have seen, modern culture experienced and had confidence in the promise of life and of the future because it believed that informed and organized intelligence, to use Dewey's phrase, could resolve our most fundamental problems. Now that such intelligence, both as science and as technology, has revealed itself as essentially ambiguous, as raising as many serious problems of survival and of well-being as it solves, the question of the meaning of our history—a philosophical and a religious question—is again forced directly upon us now by the career of a scientific and technological culture itself. Not only do the two of them reveal the reality of the bondage of our will; they disclose as well and anew the ambiguity and deep mystery of human history, the real possibility of self-generated catastrophy, and the need for a deeper basis for our confidence in the future than a confidence based only on our own virtue and wisdom. If we look carefully at the ecological evidence, the future of our scientific civilization can be presented in dark colors indeed. Despair and not confidence seems in truth to be the issue of a technological culture when it has run its full course.

A word, therefore, must be said in as sharp a contradistinction to this new despair as to that culture's former euphoric and naive optimism. Our human history is not compounded merely of human creativity and of our destructive use of that creativity, both of which science and technology have now disclosed to us. There is also—so our religious tradition affirms—the Lord who brings judgment on cultures that are too proud of their wisdom and power, who gives the possibility of repentance and of new life to those who listen to that judgment, and who—as with a captive Israel—always holds out the promise of a new covenant, a new act, a new possibility in history that may redeem the times and bring light even to the future that is coming.

7

RELIGIOUS DILEMMAS OF A SCIENTIFIC CULTURE

The title may well seem puzzling. We can easily understand that a scientific culture poses dilemmas for traditional religion, or religion of any sort. This has been assumed ever since our culture became scientific in the sixteenth and seventeenth centuries—and it became a virtual certainty in the nineteenth. But can a scientific culture as it develops raise its own religious dilemmas, show itself to be in need of religion in the way agricultural and nomadic societies were? This is the question I would like to investigate. I shall begin by exploring a middle term, *history,* and our understanding of history. For science has greatly influenced our sense of history, of where we are all going—and wishes to do so. And with the question of the meaning of history, religion inevitably enters the scene.

Generally speaking, scientists and technologists have not been directly concerned with philosophical questions about history and its meaning. In fact, the general effect of a scientific culture has been to regard speculative philosophy, and especially the philosophy of history, as about as "mythical" and full of fancy as religion and theology—and both as quite unnecessary for intelligent understanding. Nevertheless, the scientific and technological communities, despite their best intentions, so to speak, have generated out of their own abilities, commitments, and hopes a new understanding of history both reflectively and existentially, both in our thoughts and in our feelings. And almost any book by a scientist, when it speaks of the importance of science or of its role in society, reflects a particular understanding of history common to the scientific community. It is not the direct inquiries of science that have created and continue to create this philosophy of history; the latter is not a thesis experimentally tested and therefore a part of the body of scientific knowledge. Rather it is created when the scientific community thinks of its own role in history, when science reflects on itself and its knowledge, and sees itself through that knowledge as a creative force in history. A philosophy of history—and a very hopeful one—has been a presupposition, an important spiritual foundation, of the modern scientific community since its beginnings in the sixteenth century. The shattering of that spiritual base in our day has been, therefore, a crisis for the scientific community itself and for the technological culture it helped to create.

As Francis Bacon, the father of this understanding of science and of history, reiterated, greater knowledge (empirical, not speculative knowledge) leads to greater control. When men and women know the way things around them work, then they can make those things work for them. Since science leads to far greater understanding of the dynamic causes of things, science is the secret of human control over the world. Thus, with the advent of the scientific method, the deliberate, organized, and successful effort to *know,* a new day has dawned for humanity: a day of new power, the power to control and direct, the power to remake our world, the power at last to realize human purposes through intelligent inquiry and the technical control that intelligence brings. Bacon's simple empiricistic understanding of the method of science has long since been superceded; but his vision of the role of science in human society and history has remained the fundamental belief and hope of the modern scientific and technological world. Through this method, we now know how to know, and through that knowledge to control. And, as John Dewey was to point out, the two—knowing and controlling—are in the end one and the same thing, the same power of organized intelligence, as he put it, to remake its world. Science functions as the means to human power, power over nature, society, and men and woman alike. Thus, both old and developing nations have seen scientific and technological knowledge as the keys to their military power and to their economic and social well-being—and each becomes fearful for its security if its lead in pure science is threatened.

There are many evils from which we humans suffer, and almost as many interpretations of those ills, which ones are basic and which peripheral. Generally,. most profound religions have interpreted the fundamental ills as coming from the inside of the self and from its finitude: from desire, pride, disloyalty, lust, mortality, and death. Not so modernity. For most moderns, our ills have come not from inside ourselves but from threats from the outside: from our weakness and our ignorance, from our subjection to external forces beyond our present control, from our inability—in being ignorant of these forces and how they work—to control them. The disasters of nature, the problems of heat and cold, the vast spaces of nature to traverse, the difficulties of communication, the disease of the body, the paucity of necessary goods—these have been for modern technological society the basic "problems" that beset us in life. Since these are the main evils we face, then if through our knowledge we can develop tools or instruments with which to deal with them, if we can control these "fates" of disaster, hunger, disease, and want that afflict us from the outside, will we not be happy? Not only then can more of us survive, but through the technologizing of industry, we can survive securely, fully, and well—and a new kind of human life will be possible. Homo faber, the tool maker, transformed through science into technological and industrial man, is the "authentic" man because he alone can eradicate evil and bring in a new, authentic world. Of course, I have left out here these two other great issues of modernity relevant to human well-being: the distribution and control of political power and the distribution of economic goods and property. My point is, however, that whatever political or economic system we choose, this belief in science, technology, and industrialism, in verified knowledge, technical know-how, and organizational techniques, as a means of curing human ills has dominated the scene, whether we look at Europe and North America, at Russia or Rumania, at India, China, or Japan. The ultimate, long-term faith of this modern culture begun in Europe was in the scientist and his or her knowledge; but its immediate and practical hope, one may say, lay in the engineer: the builder of roads and factories, cars, tractors, and planes, apartments and cities, sanitation, detergents, and improved fertilizers. Through technological and industrial expansion, jobs are created, wants appeased, politics made stable, food production increased, economic life rendered solvent, and the power and self-determination of a people guaranteed. We all know this to be in large part true, and, when we are honest, we admit that we too welcome its results. Life on our planet can hardly survive, let alone be pleasant, without these three: science, technology, and industrialism.

Modern science and technology, then, brought with them, both reflectively and in our feelings, a message of promise for the future. A new and better world was now possible. Thus did the theory of progress arise in the seventeenth and eighteenth centuries, both among philosophers and intellectuals generally and as a cultural mood slowly shared by all, out of the role that science and technology were beginning to play and promised to play in society. The future appears on a wide scale as an important category of thought, as the "place" where this "new" will appear, as the place where the ills of the past and of the present will dissolve. Science and technology produced that understanding of history that has dominated our entire present, capitalist and Marxist alike, and has spread like fire across the globe wherever this culture has gone: the sense of an open future, of a future that will be better, the confidence in progress.

Here is the main source of the new historical consciousness characteristic of modern culture: a sense of our freedom in history to remake our world, of the possibility of the conquest of fate and evil, of human potentiality to fulfill itself and its life without either divine help or a relation to eternity. No wonder modernity, to a new generation excited with this new knowledge, has seemed to make traditional religion irrelevant and unnecessary in East and West alike. Science appeared to show that religion was incredible, a result of our childish ignorance when we did not yet understand our world or our own powers in it. But perhaps more important, science made religious salvation irrelevant now that the weakness of humanity in achieving its desires had through knowledge been changed into power, the power to control whatever it wills to control.

One further word about the new historical consciousness. A new sense of change has resulted from technology and industrialism. Men and women have always been aware of changes in nature and in themselves: the cycle of the seasons around them, and of birth, growth, and death in all that lives. And they have often been aware of confusion and chaos, of the loss of all stability in their social world: as at the end of the Roman Empire and of the Middle Ages, or in the feudal chaos before the Tokugawa period in Japan. But they have not been explicitly aware of a changing *social* world, of a transformation of the forms of life leading to something new, until modern times. Such awareness arose partly through the cataclysmic political events that overturned a seemingly changeless order: like the French Revolution in Europe and the Meiji restoration in Japan. But the deep modern awareness of steady and cumulative historical change has arisen, I believe, through the accelerated changes that technology and industrialism have effected in all our lands. Each of us sees, and feels deeply, the inexorable disappearance of the old and the appearance of the new in our social environment. Almost as if we were on a speeding railway, the world we grew up in and accustomed ourselves to flashes by at lightning speed to be replaced by new scenery, by a new world. And with that transformation of the environment by expanding cities, exploding factories, and new roads have come equally drastic changes in modes of life, in social relations, in the roles we each play in our world. All men and women have lived in time and change and have felt them. We know in a new way that we live in a historical process, a process of the steady change of the forms of our social environment and of ourselves. We are conscious in a quite new way of being immersed in history, and thus of facing tomorrow a world we may not expect or even want. It is no surprise that modern philosophy—of almost all sorts, naturalistic, idealistic, existential—has emphasized process, change, and the temporality of being as opposed to the eternity and changelessness of being. This has been the modern experience of whatever being they knew, and their philosophies have expressed this sense of the historicity of all that is.

For most people—except for those given privileges by the old order—it was with relief, joy, and expectation that the world of yesterday was disappearing and a new world of tomorrow was coming. Thus, when this sense of change first appeared, it felt good: change was promise, the promise of a new that would be better. To be in process feels good if process equals growth and progress. Change has a different feel, however, if we are not too sure whether the new will be better or not; and it is terrifying if the new appears as menacing. In any case, it is evident once again how science, technology, and industrialism as the main agents of change in our social world have generated feelings and reflections about history. They have together helped to create our historical consciousness, our awareness of our historicity and temporality: that we are what we are in historical process, that we are immersed in social change, and that we can through intelligence and will refashion, shape, and direct that change. Despite all its positivism and empiricism, its impatience with speculative philosophy and theology, at the deepest level modernity has been founded on a new philosophy of history, a philosophy built on faith in knowledge and its power to control, on the triumph through knowledge of human purposes over blind fate, and on the confidence that change, if guided by intelligence informed by inquiry, can realize human fulfillment in this life. Such a view of history as guided by science and shaped by technology was the implicit "religion" of the West until a few decades ago.

A change both in mood and in reflection, in feelings and in explicit thought, has occurred in the last decades with regard to this fundamental confidence in science and technology and all that they imply about freedom, history, and the future—like a sudden cover of storm clouds shutting out the bright sun. A chill, thematized in art, drama, novels, and films, unthematized but felt by most people, has settled over much of the West. And the scientific community in particular is uncertain about its role and worried about its future—and the future of the society it helped to create—in a way unknown before. Such anxiety appears whenever a "religious" confidence becomes shaky. The center of this new angst is, I believe, a new intuition of the ambiguity of science and technology as forces in history. This is not primarily an uncertainty about the validity of scientific knowledge or about the reliability of technological skills. On these issues there are few new doubts—except among small (but growing) mystical and religious communities in the counterculture. It is rather a radical doubt about their "saving" character and an anxious feeling that they create as many new problems and dilemmas for human life as they resolve, and even that they may compound our ills rather than dissolve them.

Back of this anxiety, but rarely explicitly expressed, lie deeper and more devastating questions. If a valid science and a reliable technology can really compound our problems rather than dissolve them, what does that mean about humanity and about the history it helps to create? Do we really increase our dilemmas by using our intelligence, our inquiry, our techniques? What does that mean about us? When these questions are asked, it becomes evident that the *user* of knowledge and technology, humanity itself, is the cause of this ambiguity. Possibly, the knowledge, informed intelligence, and the freedom to enact human purposes that they give are not enough. Something seems to be radically wrong with the ways we use our intelligence, our knowledge, and with the ways we enact our control. Can it be true that human creativity, in which we have so deeply believed, is in some strange way self-destructive, that there is in human freedom an element of the demonic, and that intelligence and informed freedom, far from exorcising the fates of history, can create their own forms of fate over which they also have no control? As is evident, all the great philosophical and especially religious problems about human life are implicitly raised here, problems unanswerable by science and unresolvable by technology, and yet raised by both of them the moment the future they seem to create becomes apparently oppressive and menacing rather than bright and promising.

As we all know, these deeper questions about scientific knowledge and control have been brewing for some time. They began with the development and use of the terrible new weapons and the threat to human life itself that the technological power evidenced in them represented. These questions continued with the realization that technology provides the political authorities and a potential scientific elite with new and dangerous powers over ordinary people: political powers based on weapons and communications systems unavailable to the people, and on the possibility of psychological and even genetic control over entire populations. Technology seemed now not so much to guarantee freedom and self-determination, individuality of style of life and privacy of personal existence—freedom from *natural* fates to become human—as it did to open up the possibility of an all-encompassing totalitarianism that could crush individuality and humanity, a submission of the human to a new kind of *social* and *historical* fate. These fears have been expressed for some decades in the Western consciousness, for example, by Huxley and Orwell. However, two new factors have recently become visible that have widely increased this uneasiness about a technological culture: one of them since World War II and the other in the last decade.

The first can be referred to as the dehumanizing effects of a technological culture. As Jacques Ellul has pointed out, technology is not only a matter of tools, instruments, machines, and computers. It also characterizes a *society* insofar as it is organized, systematized, or rationalized into an efficient organization: as in an army, an efficient business, or a bureaucracy. Here, all the human parts are integrated with each other into a practical, efficient, smooth-running organization where no time, effort, or materials are wasted; the product or the service is quickly, correctly, and inexpensively created; and a minimum of loss, error and cross-purposes is achieved. Thus are identical homes built by a single company and according to a single plan—for efficiency's sake; thus is local government submerged in national bureaucracy; thus do individual farms give way to farming combines; and thus is every small industry swallowed up by large, unified business or state concerns. The beneficial results of this technologizing or rationalizing of society are obvious: the rising standards of living of America, Europe, and Japan have directly depended on the development of this sort of efficient, centralized administration of industry, distribution, services, and government. And every developing country seeks to increase as rapidly as possible its rationalization of production and organization in order to feed, clothe, house, and defend its people.

In the midst of these benefits, however, there have appeared other, negative consequences. As every advanced technological society has discovered, human beings are now not so much masters as the servants of the organizations they have created, servants in the sense that they find themselves "caught" and rendered inwardly helpless within the system insofar as they participate in it at all. By this I mean that they experience their personness, their individuality, their unique gifts, creativity, and joy—their sense of their own being and worth—as sacrificed to the common systematic effort, an effort in which all that their own thought and ingenuity can contribute is to devise more practical means to an uncriticized end. Any considerations they might raise concerning creativity, aesthetics, or the moral meaning of what is being done, that might compromise the efficiency, the smooth running of the whole team, are "impracticable" and so irrational. Thus does the individuality of each lose its transcendence over the system; their minds and consciences cease to be the masters and become its servants, devoted only to its harmony and success. Human beings are here, and are creative, only as parts of a system; their worth is judged only with regard to their contribution as an efficient part; they are lured into being merely parts of a machine.

The system has, moreover, proved ruthlessly destructive of many of the other, less public grounds of our identity as persons. It uproots us from that in which much of our identity, or sense of it, is founded, namely, our identification with a particular place and with a particular community. For it gathers us into ever-larger groups of people similarly organized, and then it moves us about from here to there, from these people to those, within the larger society. It rewards and satisfies us only externally by giving us things to consume or to watch. After all, such things are all that efficient organization can produce. Having dampened our creative activity in the world into the rote work expected of a mere part of a system, it now smothers the intensity of our private enjoyments by offering us the passive pleasures of mere consumption. Thus does it stifle our inwardness.

Ironically, the West had in its spiritual career discovered and emphasized, as had no other culture, the reality, uniqueness, and value of the inwardness of each human being, of what was once called the "soul." But a concurrent theme, its affirmation of the goodness of life, the intelligibility of the world, and the possibility through knowledge of the latter's manipulation and control has gradually achieved an almost exclusive dominance. The combination of these two themes had promised to reshape human existence in relation both to nature and to the forms of social life, culminating in technology, democracy, and socialism. Thus, in comparison with the Eastern world, the West had creatively learned to manipulate the external, objective world and done much to humanize and rationalize the objective social order. But it has in the process endangered its own inward soul, the reality and creativity of the spirit. Thus, having through science, technology, democracy, and socialism helped to rescue the Orient's social orders, it now must turn back to the Orient in order to rediscover its own inwardness. And it is doing so in great numbers—ironically, just when the Orient is itself grasping after the lures of Western technology and external progress!

Technological society promised to free the individual from crushing work, from scarcity, disease, and want, to free him or her to become himself or herself by dispensing with these external fates. In many ways, on the contrary, it has—or threatens to do so—emptied rather than freed the self by placing each person in a homogeneous environment, setting him or her as a replaceable part within an organized system, and satisfying external wants rather than energizing creative powers. Thus appears the first paradox: the organization of modern society necessary to the survival and well-being of the race seems now to menace the humanity, the inwardness, and creativity of the race. In seeking to live by means of a surplus of goods unknown before and for the sake of such goods, we find that men and women are in danger of losing themselves inwardly and so of dying in the process. What had been seen clearly with regard to individual life by the wisdom of every religious tradition has been proved objectively on a vast scale by modern consumer culture: men and women cannot live by bread alone.

Consciousness of the second menacing face of technology is astoundingly recent, within the last half-decade. This may be termed the "ecology" crisis in its widest connotations. It refers not only to the problems of technological and industrial pollution of the water, air, and earth, and the despoliation of whatever natural beauties are left—though these are serious enough problems, and with energy and resources in short supply will only get worse—but it also refers centrally to the exhaustion through expanded industrial production of the earth's available resources, in the end a far more serious problem. Medicine and greater production of food have increased the population; technology in both agriculture and industry has at an accelerating pace increased our use of nature's resources of fuels, metals and chemicals. In order to feed and care for that mounting population, such agricultural and industrial growth must itself expand almost exponentially. And yet if it does, an absolute limit or term will soon be reached; these resources will come to an end, if not in two or three generations, then surely in four or five. The seemingly infinite expansion of civilization and its needs is in collision course with the obstinate finitude of available nature and threatens to engulf both civilization and nature. For the first time, our freedom in history menaces not only our fellow humans but nature as well. In the past, with the development of the techniques of civilization, history was freed from the overwhelming power of nature and its cycles and submitted nature to her own control. Now civilization and history have become so dominant in their power that they threaten to engulf nature in their own ambiguity.

In this case, that ambiguity is very great. A world economy, whether its domestic forms be socialist or capitalist, facing the combination of expanded populations and depleted and diminishing resources, is a world facing even more bitter rivalries and conflicts than the past has known. It is also, ironically, a world facing in new forms precisely these "fates" from which technology had promised to save us: scarcity, crowding, want, and undue authority. If there are to be rational solutions to these problems impinging on us from the future, and there are, they will require an immense increase in corporate planning and control on a world scale: control of technological developments, of the industrial use of natural resources, of distribution, of the wide disparities of the use and consumption of resources. Freedom of experiment, freedom for new and radical thoughts and techniques, freedom for individual life-styles may well be unaffordable luxuries in that age. Perhaps most important, such rational and peaceful solutions will require from the nations with power an extraordinary self-restraint in the use of their power, a willingness for the sacrifice of their affluence lest they be tempted to use their power to grab all that is left for the sake of that affluence. All of this bespeaks an increase of authority in our future undreamed of in the technological utopias of the recent past. Whether we will or no, we seem headed for a less free, less affluent, less individualistic, less dynamic, and innovative world. The long-term results of science and technology seem ironically to be bringing about anything but the individualistic, creative, secure world they originally promised. In fact, this progressive, dynamic, innovative civilization seems to be in the process of generating its own antithesis: a stable, even stagnant society with an iron structure of rationality and authority, with a minimum of goods, of self-determination, of intellectual and personal freedom. Such a grim world is by no means a certainty, for nothing in history is fated. But unless our public life—technical, political, and economic—is directed by more reason and more self-sacrifice than in the past, such a future has a disturbingly high probability.

As the hope latent in science and technology gave birth despite themselves to a new understanding of history, so the new sense of their ambiguity raises for us a host of unavoidable questions about history and the relation of human freedom—of human intelligence, will, and creativity—to history. Technology, along with language, is itself one of the most vivid manifestations of human freedom over its immediate environment. And, as we have seen, its growth in modernity has sparked the consciousness of that freedom in history, the ability of humankind to remake its world. And yet, paradoxically, technology in the long run seems not so much creative of the freedom it represents as destructive of it, for it seems to be creating conditions that will of necessity absorb freedom into authority. Here, the exercise of technical freedom in order to remove the fates that determine freedom from the outside has itself become a fate that menaces freedom—a strange ending.

Again, paradoxically, this most vivid manifestation of freedom has exacerbated industrial expansion that in turn ravishes and desecrates nature, that spurs us all to rivalry, conflict, and doom. Under and behind the creativity of humanity, recently so clear to the modern West as the principle of historical salvation, lies the estrangement and the demonic principle within us—whatever our ideals, our loyalties, our courage, and ingenuity. Finally, and most ironical of all, man as the tool maker, as inquirer and technologist, has by modern savants been regarded as the paradigm of survival. He, not religious, mystical or mythical man, was the "practical" one who alone could handle "reality." Strangely, now Homo faber, as technologist supreme, seems himself to be alienated from "reality," bringing about through his technology his own self-destruction and showing himself to be the primary danger to the survival of his race. No more startling contradiction to the spirit of modernity from the Enlightenment to the present could be conceived.

Thus has what we can only call the mystery of history and of temporal being revealed itself to us anew, and the potential of meaninglessness in the human story, as well as in individual life. Human creativity—yes, even informed intelligence and good purposes—is no simple "god" bringing to us unadulterated blessings, the answers to our every wish. With our creativity freeing us from old fates comes fate in a new form; with our creativity the demonic seems to be continually reintroduced into history. We live in a far stranger and more disturbing history than we thought, where even our apparent victories, our most cherished mastery, our greatest intellectual and practical triumphs help to seal our doom!

I need not in conclusion underline that these paradoxes arising out of the role of science and technology in modern life raise religious issues. It is obvious that all these questions make direct contact with the themes, meanings, questions, and answers of speculative philosophy and high religion. If it is our creativity and not its lack that is at fault, if it be the way we use our intelligence and freedom—not our lack of either—then is there any resource for us from this estrangement of our own most treasured and precious powers? From this bondage of our wills to self-destruction? We seem to need rescue not so much from our ignorance and our weakness as from our own creative strength—not so that either our creativity or intelligence is lost, but so that their self-destructive power is gone. Thus, the religious question of a ground of renewal, not from ourselves but from beyond ourselves, is raised by the most impressive of modernity's achievements, its scientific intelligence, and its technological capacities. The creative role of religion is not to replace intelligence and technology with something else, but to enable us to be more intelligent, more rational, more self-controlled, more just in our use of them. Further, if it is our creativity itself which threatens the meaning of our history—because it renders ambiguous our common future—then again the question of a meaning in history which is more than the meaning which we can create or give to history appears. In the face of the fate with which our own creativity seems able to dominate us, the religious question arises whether there is any other providence that can rule these fates that seem to rule over us. Our history and our future are not threatened by the stars or the blind gods—by forces beyond us. Ironically, they are threatened by a fate which our own freedom and ingenuity have themselves created. Here too, therefore, for us to be able to face our future with confidence—for we can no more live without technology than we can apparently live humanely with it—we must trust in a power that tempers and transmutes the evil that is in our every good and the unreason that is in our highest intelligence.

Such issues as these, raised not *against* science and technology but precisely by them, cannot be understood or even discussed without religious categories. Moreover, on the existential as well as on the reflective level, they cannot be dealt with without a confidence and a trust born of religion. The anxieties involved in facing such a potentially menacing future require the serenity, the courage, and the willingness to sacrifice that only touch with the transcendent can bring. Modern culture in developing its science and technology thought it made religion irrelevant. It has made religious understanding and the religious spirit more necessary than ever if we are to be human, and even if we are to survive. Technology by itself, technical manipulative reason, if made the exclusive form of reason and of creativity, has been clearly shown to possess a built-in element that leads to its own destruction and the destruction of all it manipulates. It must be complemented by humanity's religious dimension and by the participating, uniting function of reason if it, and we, are to survive at all.

Specifically, it is not with regard to their own modes of inquiry, their conclusions, or even their specific programs that science, technology, and the society they together form must be tempered and shaped by the religious dimension of humanity—though the latter do need ethical as well as practical assessment. Rather this tempering and shaping has to do with the humans who use them and on whom they are used. From religion alone has traditionally come the concern with the human that can prevent the manipulation of people and the dehumanization of society; and from religion alone can come the vision or conception of the human that can creatively guide social policy. From religious confidence alone has come the courage in the face of fate and despair—especially when these last two arise from the distortion of our own creativity—to confront a future that will by no means be easier than the past. For humanism can count on only our own deepest creativity; when that reveals itself as ambiguous, then despair and cynicism rather than humanistic confidence appear. From religion alone can come the healing of desire and concupiscence, that demonic driving force behind our use of technology that ravishes the world. And from religion alone can come a new understanding of the unity of nature, history, and humankind—not in human subservience to nature and her cycles, but in an attitude which, recognizing the unique spiritual creativity of humankind, can still find human life a dependent part of a larger spiritual whole that includes the natural world on which we depend. Such a unity with nature has been expressed in much traditional religion, especially in the Orient. It must be reexpressed and reintegrated in light of the modern consciousness of human freedom, of technological possibilities, and of history. Naturalistic humanism cannot achieve such a unity with nature through spirit. Without the category of the ultimate, the transcendent, or the divine, beyond and yet inclusive of both nature and human being, we are either subordinated to nature or, recognizing our transcendence, use her for our own "superior" ends. Thus religion is necessary in a technological society if such a society and the nature on which it depends are to survive.

But—and religion both East and West should take note—it is only a religion related to history, to social existence, and to the human in its social and historical context that can complement, shape, and temper technology. A religion that lifts us out of time or gives us only individual peace, that vacates society and history in favor of transcendence alone, will only encourage an irresponsible and demonic technology and will foster and not conquer a sense of fate within history. We are, whether we will or no, *in* history, immersed in historical and social process; and here our lives, for good or ill, are led. On our response to the destiny of our time—in this case a technological destiny of vast ambiguity—rests the validity and meaning of our spiritual life, of our religion. Only a religion that responds to a transcendence beyond our own self-destructive powers and yet that finds its task centered in our common historical and social future can become a genuine means of grace to us.

8

IS RELIGIOUS FAITH POSSIBLE
IN AN AGE OF SCIENCE?

The question in this title is a fundamental one. It represents, let us note, as much a question about the characteristics and needs of human beings and their history as it does a query about faith or religion. For the question—is faith possible in an age of science—implies that with an age of science a basic change has taken place in the status and needs of human beings, a change that renders religion suddenly very problematic. Whereas before, in primitive and traditional societies, religion seemed a very understandable phenomenon, now it may well not be at all. In the older world—so this modern viewpoint runs—knowledge was so scanty, instruments and techniques so primitive, and thus the existence of men and women so vulnerable, that they needed religious faith to give them courage, guidance, and hope. Now, however, with our new ability to know, to understand, and to control, our status in the world and in history has been fundamentally altered; we have matured, "come of age," are now on our own as never before, competent through our knowledge, our skills, and our techniques to direct our communal and personal life without untested beliefs or commitments, without uncriticized ultimates, without an awesome sacred—without the burden of religious authority and the "false consciousness" of faith. This view, therefore, sees an age of faith and an age of science as mutually exclusive alternatives. It is against this background that we who still represent that old eon raise the question, is faith possible in an age of science?

I shall seek to address this question on this wider level, as a question about the role of faith and the religious within human cultural and historical existence generally, and within a scientific epoch specifically. But if this general question shapes my approach, I must in these remarks use the categories "faith" and "the religious" in a wider, less specific sense than we usually intend them, when "faith" means Christian faith and "religion" means the Christian or possibly the Jewish religion. One consequence of the use of a more general sense of faith and the religious is, of course, that any arguments about their necessity, inevitability, or possibility are not arguments for the cogency or validity of any specific form of faith—though by the same token they are arguments for the possibility or potential value of specific religions.

My argument, then, will maintain that in an age of science faith or the religious in their most general sense are first inescapable, secondly necessary, and thus thirdly fully possible. And that finally, as a consequence of such an inevitable role, certain requirements are set for the religious within an age of science to which, it seems to me, the Christian faith is eminently appropriate and adequate, though the latter point represents more of a hint, a personal flourish at the end, so to speak, than it does an explicated argument.

This whole case does not deny but builds upon the undeniable fact of change in the role of traditional religious institutions and beliefs in recent cultural history. There is no doubt that in the modern epoch traditional religion has steadily lost that central and dominating social and personal role that it possessed in "Christendom" as well as in archaic societies, and that this recession from the center is partly due to the appearance and gradual dominance of science and technology. This change in the social role of traditional religion has had two major results relevant to our theme: (1) the religious has begun to appear in other modes and guises, and (2) traditional religious communities have been encouraged, or forced, to rethink, reinterpret, and revise their structures, their role, their beliefs—their most basic self-understanding. Religions do change, as do education, science, politics, and economic life. Our courses in theology are as different from seventeenth-century curricula in dogmatics as are courses at a modern medical school from lectures on bleeding in earlier medical history! While such change in the forms of religion is itself partly an aspect of the age of science, such change does not at all entail the disappearance, the insignificance, or the irrelevance of the religious in our age. I need not point out how central to contemporary political, social, and cultural history such changes in the religious have been and are, and what explosive results they may have, whether we look towards Rome and Tübingen, Jerusalem and Damascus, Mecca and Teheran—or even to the contemporary temples and shrines in Peking, Moscow, and Washington! In each of these centers, and in many more, our age is witnessing epic struggles over precisely this reduced role of religion, over the process of the revision or reinterpretation of religion, and over the reappearance of the religious in new, often creative, and yet also potentially demonic forms.

My first thesis, then, is that faith and its sibling, the religious, appear to be inescapable, even—perhaps especially—in an age of science. Let me illustrate this through pointing to two phenomena, both unexpected to our modern self-understanding, but apparently characteristic of a scientific, technological, and industrial society, namely, the rise of ideologies to communal dominance and the recent proliferation of novel religious cults.

It is no accident that the word *ideology,* and the reality to which it seeks to refer, first surface right after the French Revolution, which, among other things, removed traditional religion from its place in the center of European political, social, and spiritual life. Ideology has been variously defined, as we all know; certain common elements accrue to all its variations. First, it refers to a global system of ideas or symbols which give shape to the whole of history and so of social reality, and thus which place the community holding the ideology, its life, its prospects, and its unique character on the wider stage of universal destiny, and so which give that community its vocation or special task in history. It is a Weltanschauung with a social base and a communal function. Secondly, ideology, as both Napoleon and Marx used the term, has a pejorative sense: it connotes a claim on the truth that is unwarranted, or, (as Alvin Gouldner points out) in Marx's usage against classical economics, a claim to be "objective" and "scientific." Thus, religion, making no such claim to be "science," was not originally considered to be an example of ideology. For Marx, moreover, this claim hides some form of self-interest, the interest of a person but more probably of a group; in an ideology a set of ideas about reality both masks and assists a group's grasp for power or retention of power. Thus, when we use the word ideology about some other group, we signal a disdain of their ideas as empty and yet also, so to speak, as armed to the teeth; we are at once both scornful and wary—as the eighteenth-century philosophes were of organized religion, of priests, and of presbyters, and as we might be of the Ayatollah. Thirdly, as the symbolic structure uniting and directing a society's life, an ideology must be spiritually, inwardly, and unconditionally participated in by the members of the group to be effective, and for the group to be effective. That participation has two aspects: intellectual assent to the validity of the symbolic structure of the ideology and commitment to the obligations of that structure as binding on the self. Thus is Russia, much like older "religious" communities, worried about dissidents and revisionists, and so intent on control of thought, of education, of publications, and of art: thus are our corresponding ideologues upset at each domestic criticism or qualification of the "American Way of Life"—"Love America or Leave It" expresses this demand both for unconditional inward assent and for loyalty.

I need not press, I am sure, the important implications of this analysis of the modern phenomenon of ideology. First, it is evident that ideologies have appeared in an age of science and have clearly replaced traditional religions as the essential and apparently necessary symbolic systems of modern technological societies; not surprisingly, in a scientific society they tend to base their claim to allegiance on their status as "objective science" rather than as divinely revealed or traditionally sacrosanct. Strangely, as debates between the social theorists of capitalism and those of communism show, each calling the other "nonscientific" and so "ideological," each modern ideology appears to its adherents as science, to its opponents as the very opposite of science—and to those of us who observe them, as providing the presupposed *ground* of science, namely that socially oriented Weltanschauung on which each form of modern scientific, technological culture rests.

Secondly, the lineaments or anatomy of ideologies, from their beginning in the eighteenth century to the present, have evidently a *religious* character to them. They are not "religions." Nevertheless, they clearly have religious aspects or dimensions: the claim to ultimacy, the deep relatedness to the normative, the requirement of faith or commitment, the fear of heterodoxy and apostasy, the ritual rites and mythologies, the fleets of theologians and missionaries (the latter called "information bureaus"). Finally, these social faiths or ideologies are productive at once of all relevant social theory and yet also of most destructive social bias. Thus, they pose some of the major socially relevant theoretical and philosophical issues of our time, as the predominance of "ideology-critique" in European social philosophy and political theology indicates. Here in this new form, a scientific age encounters in its social debates many of the classical theoretical and practical problems of traditional religious theory: how is an affirmation of truth possible if relativism be admitted; how are tolerance, charity, and love possible—or are they even wanted—between ultimate faiths; how far is heresy to be admitted in any society; how is continuous and basic self-criticism possible within any social body that affirms its cherished beliefs, values, and norms? In modern societies where science has become a dominant force there are few traditional religions that direct and control, as they once did, public life and discussion. Nevertheless, the issues with which in an age of religion religious symbols and theory once dealt, and the modalities of religious thinking and speaking, have returned in a new secular garb and are once again at the center of human communal existence. Modern societies structured around an ideological center have replaced archaic societies structured around a religious center; an implicit religious dimension has taken the place of an explicit one. The differences between the societies of these wildly disparate epochs are real and significant— but the similarities are equally so, and much more unexpected.

I shall not discuss in any detail the second surprising reappearance of the religious, and of faith as its correlate, within a scientific culture, namely, the rise to new prominence of religious cults and movements. Here we speak not of implicit religion, of religious *aspects* of cultural life; rather we point to groups and movements based purely on religious impulses, religious power, and religious goals. These too have grown and prospered in our time; in fact, so much so that one is tempted to say they have flourished not in spite of a scientific culture but because of it! Moreover, such a manifestation of the purely religious has occurred on all levels of our society. The astounding growth of conservative or fundamentalist Christian groups is one indication. When I lived in Nashville, Tennessee, Huntsville, Alabama was to me an important clue of the paradoxical, complex character of a developed technological society. Here at the national center of technological expertise, at the site of the most advanced space engineering, missile sheds and fundamentalist churches, acres of technical drawing boards and gospel pulpits, existed side by side and yet in the closest conjunction. To either a philosopher of science or a theologian this interdependence was a mystery—but there weren't too many of either in Huntsville!

Making their appearance on the scene a bit later, esoteric religious and even magical groups—some devoted to meditation, some to new religious styles of life and worship, some bizarrely supernatural—have sprung up in every urban center, but particularly in Berkeley, Hyde Park, Cambridge, and Manhattan. Thus, it is noteworthy that these esoteric groups clearly huddle around, in, and about the great universities of our time and so are functions not of the "ignorant" but precisely of the intelligentsia. In the case of both fundamentalism and the cults—as well as in the proliferation of new self-help groups in middle-class life—we find the religious flourishing in the area of personal life, providing answers to the personal search for identity, self-discipline, certainty of belief, self-understanding, confidence, serenity, and perhaps an experience of ecstasy. These are clearly commitments that in no way conflict with scientific or technical work; a graduate student in natural science, possibly even in psychology, can practice Yoga at the deepest spiritual level and find no conflict. Equally clearly, the scientific and technological culture has neither eradicated nor answered whatever personal, inward, or communal needs these groups may fill, as was once expected.

As ideologies rushed in to fill the void left in the separation of church and state, of religion from objective society, so personal religion in evangelical or cultic form has arisen to give structure and meaning to personal life in a centerless, industrialized world. As the life of society has become more technological and its official academic and intellectual existence steadily more empirical and positivistic, the religious has not thereby gone away—nor will it. Rather it reappears *alongside* the technical and the rational; and then (this is its sneaky, dangerous side) it ends up governing and controlling, making servants of the technical and the theoretical. We can see this over and over in the lives of individuals; our century has seen it even more vividly on the grand scale as whole societies have found their scientific, technological, and industrial might used in the service of their own reigning ideology. We may think that our pragmatic, liberal, "free" society in America, precisely because it is pragmatic, is for that reason free of all this; it is, however, well to realize that for the *same* reason other communities judge us to be one of the prime examples of contemporary ideological bondage!

The facts seem to indicate, then, that even in an age of science, faith and the religious are inescapable, reappearing in different guises and, as always, taking a major role in communal and personal life. If the religious thus is inescapable, even in a culture that sought to disavow and dissolve its dominance, it would seem that the religious is essential, even necessary. Human being appears to be "religious" in some important dimension of its being, much as it is sexual, social, political, economic, linguistic, humorous, tool making. Our task, then, is to try to understand this, to make explicit, if we can, why it is and how it is that the religious represents an essential dimension in human being. If we can do this, we may be able to understand more precisely how it may be that religious faith can be said to be a "possibility" even in our age.

There are in human life, individual and social, certain kinds of very significant, even ultimate questions and issues which arise, which cannot easily be avoided, and yet which seem difficult to answer or unravel. With these issues, our ordinary modes of inquiry tend to break down, certainty of any sort is hard to establish, and clarity and precision are elusive if not almost absent. Gabriel Marcel helpfully called these "mysteries" instead of "puzzles." These have also been called "limit questions," questions beyond the limits of our ordinary methods and beyond the possibilities of verifiable knowledge. They have also been called "limit questions" because each one seems to appear at the outer limits of our capacities and powers, at the edge, so to speak, of our finitude. And they have been called "ultimate questions" because of their importance, their unavoidability, and because answers to them are foundational for all else we are and do. I suggest, at least for the purposes of this study and for reasons that will become clear, that we also call them "religious questions." If we can locate them, understand their inescapability, their elusiveness, and yet their basic role in our life, we may be able better to understand why the religious appears so consistently and in so many forms, even in our own age.

As we go through these limit questions, let us note two things about them. First, answers to them form a large part of the content of the ideologies I described earlier and also a large part of the religious myths and symbol systems of traditional religions. Thus, it is answers to *these* questions that structure the religious symbols to which assent is given, to which commitment is offered, and which provide the norms and ultimate viewpoint characteristic of a community governed by an ideology or a traditional religion. In uncovering these limit questions, therefore, we are tracking down and identifying the gestalt or content of the religious, those symbolic structures that are the object of religious faith whether that faith be secular and ideological or traditional. Since, as we shall note, these questions appear at the edges, latent within the bases, of all political and economic debates, as well as in questions of personal identity and morals, one can understand why politics, ideology, and religion have always been so closely associated with one another, both in traditional and in contemporary cultures.

Secondly, we shall also note that each of these questions represents a major "dilemma" for our time; each is both a burning public question pressing for an answer and a mortal threat to our common life. Another unexpected character of our age of science is that its own inherent process of development has increasingly posed deep and searing *religious* dilemmas. These dilemmas are familiar in the discussions and issues of traditional religious thought, and yet they manifest themselves to us afresh and in new forms right out of the midst of our current technological, economic, political, and social matrix. My point is that modern life, at the very center of its concerns, asks the questions and suffers from the dilemmas that have characterized the religious existence of humans all through their history. Answers on *this* level are both foundational for the cultural and spiritual life of modernity—as they have been for communities and persons of all epochs—and they are in character, function, and language "religious" answers. At the deepest level of our life, we seem no different from other ages, except that the forms that our concerns and our convictions take have, as is appropriate, shifted, becoming the forms of concern and conviction of an advanced scientific and technological age.

We shall begin with two questions that surface as the moral issues foundational for any relevant present-day political, economic, and social theory, and so as the moral dilemmas threatening our common social future. The first concerns the use and abuse of power. Our scientific, technological culture has possessed a fairly naïve view of power and its usage. The human problem, so many within that culture thought, was ignorance combined with powerlessness. But new knowledge is power, said Francis Bacon; an increase of knowledge will thus increase our power to control; and with that increment of power, men and women can and will make their life better in every relevant realm. Bacon was quite right that an increase in scientific knowledge results in vast increases in technological and industrial power. However, he and the modernity that followed him had no inkling of the deep ambiguity of all human power, even power gained through objective knowledge. As our generation has discovered, the power to control can mean the power to dominate, to exploit, and ultimately the power to destroy. What is most obviously creative about us—our intelligence and our ingenuity, our freedom to understand, to manipulate, and to control our environment—ironically has created for us not freedom at all but the threat of a new destructive fate. For it has created forms of power seemingly quite beyond our rational or moral, that is, our political, control. With its vast new powers, an advanced scientific culture faces a limit question, a deep moral dilemma, a point where its own creative capabilities seem overwhelmed, enfeebled, and helpless: it faces in effect the moral and ultimately the religious question of its own *self-control* if it would use and not abuse its new power.

The second moral question that leads towards and turns into a limit or religious question is that of *authentic community,* the question of justice and the bonds of community. Much modern thought had conceived that since our major problem is caused by a lack of goods, therefore an increase of goods, made possible by technology and industrialism, could well lead to more justice, deeper community, and a better life for all. But the open sores of poverty still fester in the most affluent societies; the specter of injustice, either economic or political, still haunts even those societies, for example, America and Russia, dedicated to freedom and equality. And even those communities that have set out to resolve the issues of injustice at home find themselves willingly and yet unwillingly exploiting other societies in the wider world community. The question of the nature of authentic community remains unresolved and explosive, the issue that divides our most important ideologies. And the mode of achieving authentic community appears fully as elusive in scientific and industrial society as it was in an agricultural one. The moral dilemmas, those seemingly opposing, even contradictory values and goals—of security and justice, individual freedom and the common good, freedom and order, peace and genuine community—seem as sharp and painful in a scientific society as in any other; and the norms and symbols expressive of the resolution of these contradictions seem just as crucial and yet just as distant from realization. The religious question of authentic community, and the religious symbol of the Kingdom, suddenly appear out of the issues raised by a scientific culture as central and very relevant demands on our life as well as objects of our necessary hope.

Closely connected with these moral dilemmas that spring directly out of our technological and social life are two further questions that are perhaps less moral than metaphysical in nature. These are the question of the character and direction of historical process and the question of the relation of that process to nature. I wish here to emphasize the existential/political side of these questions rather than their speculative or philosophical implications, though the two sides cannot be separated.

Each ideology binding a community together does so by providing an identity and a goal for that community, a task in the world that gives that community "place" and confidence in its life and activities. This fundamental identity and goal—for example the "American Way of Life" and its perceived meaning for wider history—enlivens and directs the community's common actions into the future. Thus, each ideology sets its relevant community into wider history, envisions a *pattern* to that wider history and the role of that community in that pattern, and thus gives identity, task, and value to the community's life. Communist ideology and liberal-progressive ideology, however much they may differ, alike present before the eyes of their respective communities a picture of the whole of history, a picture of the central place of that special community within that vision of the whole, and thus they provide meaning for the community's life. Through the help of its ideology each of these modern communities is enabled to see its life as one in intrinsic and special relation to the very grain itself of history, history's ultimate sovereign force or forces and history's principle of meaning—much as ancient China saw herself as Tchung Kuo, the Kingdom centered directly under Heaven, and as Japan saw itself as the realm ruled by the sons and grandsons of the Sun Goddess. In the same way, the modern concepts or myths of the Material Dialectic or of liberal Progress express the claim to a special relationship with the deepest dynamic, sovereign forces of history and so to history's essential meaning. Such a relation to ultimate power and meaning seems necessary for a culture if it is to have creative elan, serenity in the face of adversity, and confident hope for the future; it clearly is a "religious" relation, one based on faith and commitment and with an unconditioned, sovereign object. But recently our age, largely through the unresolved dilemmas just rehearsed, has begun to lose its faith in the ideal vision of progress and our own role in relation to it which made up our civil religion. This loss of confidence in the ultimacy and sacrality of our own way of life poses for us a religious dilemma at the most fundamental level, and it will engender a very deep anxiety. The necessity for a renewed and refashioned vision of process and a newly based confidence in history is here evident.

Even more pressing is the problem of nature. Our power to control, manipulate, and exploit nature has increased to the point where we can now endanger nature. The final irony or ambiguity of a scientific culture is that its most obvious creativity, its technical dominance over nature, has become a threat to its life—for even this culture remains human and creaturely, contingent, and for all its power, utterly dependent on the nature that gave it birth and that sustains its precarious life. So entranced have modern men and women become with their new power and control that they have forgotten—or overlooked, and here our religious traditions were also of very little help—their participation in nature's systematic order and vitality and their dependence on her. Officially, scientific naturalism has insisted that we are only more complex *parts* of nature; but the existential and political message, the effective message, that natural science has given us is that we transcend an objectified, soulless nature as knowers of her mysteries and manipulators of her causal sequences, and thus that we are free to use that objectified realm for our own purposes as we will.

The preservation of nature is, to be sure, in large part a matter of wise, if elusive, industrial, economic, and political policy. But wisdom here is itself a function of *ethos,* of fundamental cognitive and affective attitudes to nature, and so of our deepest spiritual relatedness to ourselves, to nature, and to reality itself through each of them. Thus, as Stephen Toulmin has shown, the question of a religious cosmology is the most important present question of cognitive science; and the question of our affective relation to nature one of the most important issues on the agenda of education and the arts. This is at base, I think, also a religious issue in the strictest sense of that word. If the objectified natural world as known by science and the human world with its cultural powers and values make up the *entire* relevant universe, if they are "all that is the case," then one of these two will always be subordinate to the other. Human values, if emphasized, will set the human above and superior to nature, and then, granted our infinite greed, the human will dominate, subdue, and exploit nature. Only if there be a transcendent power and meaning that manifests itself within and through *both* realms, uniting them in their distinctive creatureliness, order, creativity, and power, can an appropriate harmony between them be found—as both the Chinese und the Japanese traditions can show us. A new theology of nature must unite itself with a new religious cosmology if such attitudes are to be given expression and to mature among us. Here, let us note, is an ancient religious and philosophical problem raised anew and in a quite novel form by a scientific culture, a problem utterly essential to its continued being.

The final two religious issues, mortality and estrangement, I will only mention. They are as problems for existence and for reflection character-istic of every culture and epoch, our own included—though that has often been forgotten. They are also the subject of every profound reli-gious philosophy and theology, and so in a variety of forms they are familiar to us all. In this context we can see that these two permeate and give final expression to each of the religious dilemmas and religious questions I have just outlined. My reference is, as I said, to the question of our finitude and so of our mortality on the one hand, and to the question, on the other, of our estrangement, our alienation from our-selves and from others which each religion recognizes in its own way and which our tradition has understood as "sin." These two, finitude and estrangement, lie back of and permeate the deepest dilemmas of a scientific culture, as they form the pervasive issues dominating every religious tradition. In this way is religion in all its forms essentially related to culture; the religious provides that most fundamental base on which a culture lives in the face of its continual and its deepest dilem-mas, and in the face of those threats to its being and meaning which are ever-present to its life. There is every indication that on this level a scientific culture, despite its vast knowledge and power, in fact *because* of them, reveals at each moment both its finitude, its dependence, and its fear of death, and also its pervasive estrangement from its own hopes and norms. Thus, it is in no way free of either of these final limit questions about its life, nor is it independent of appropriate answers to these questions.

Let me in this concluding part say something, first, about the relation to one another of science and religion if the role of religion be conceived as I have here tried to picture it; and, secondly, what sort of require-ments such a role seems to set for religion—and so for the Christian religion—in the future.

Our age has also been described as the age of the *end* of the conflict of science and religion, if each be properly understood. I agree with that, though the peace may be that of Afghanistan, that is one of conquest and subjugation, or it may be that of détente, a precarious truce at best. Let us begin with the side of religion. If our discussion of what religious symbols are about and how they function is recalled, it will be seen that, firstly, religious symbols express or give conceptual shape to the deepest moral, metaphysical, and existential dilemmas of a community's life and, secondly, that they express those creative and yet global answers to these dilemmas from which the community lives. These are, as we have seen, questions about reality (about nature and history), about order and meaning (knowledge and justice), and about redemption and reunion. In our Christian theological tradition, these questions in the end all center about God; still, as was evident, such questions and answers can be molded by a quite different set of symbolic forms, as in other religious traditions, or in humanistic or Marxist views of progress. In each case, those symbolic forms—as dilemmas and as answers—were seen to permeate down and form the basis of the cognitive, legal, moral, artistic, economic, and personal aspects of a community's life. Thus are they of crucial importance for every facet of a culture's creative existence. Yet when they are functioning creatively they do not, and certainly should not, communicate or determine particular scientific knowledge, particular legal forms, specific moral obligations, or a specific artistic style. In this sense, religious symbols are genuinely limiting matters, presuppositions at best, the background, horizon, or foundation of human existence, not sections of its immediate foreground. Religion came into conflict with science when it interpreted its traditional symbolic content as also describing that foreground, as informing us through its revelation of empirical facts in astronomy, geology, biology; as legislating authoritatively for daily customs and legal structures; as providing its own account of history's sequence of events. Under the creative criticism of a scientific culture, this authoritative role was in turn itself criticized and refashioned by religion, the meaning and validity of a religious symbol were reconceived, and the role of religion in communal and personal life refashioned. This reinterpretation in the light of an autonomous science and a humanistic culture—and yet retaining its theonomous, theistic, and christological base—has provided most of the task, the excitement, and the risk of modern Christian theology.

From the side of science, two reinterpretations of science have appeared—in almost as grudging and slow a process as the reformation of religion just referred to! First of all, natural science has *also* by its own developments been forced to reinterpret its own concepts and language as symbolic. Previous to this century, much as it was once assumed that revelation could inform us of the age of the earth, so it was then assumed that the models and concepts of physical science represented literal editions of reality "out there," and thus that objective reality corresponded to the objectified, physical, mechanical—and vacuous—models the scientists then used. Within this century, however, it has been seen that scientific concepts are abstractions for certain purposes $\leftarrow$ and based on a certain limited range of experience, abstractions set within the limiting terms of human models, and thus abstractions from a much richer and more "mysterious" reality than our most reliable methods of inquiry can capture or our pictures encompass. This does not, to be sure, challenge the reliability or the relevance of scientific knowledge; it only serves to relativize its former claim to absoluteness and sufficiency. Nor does it prove the idealistic thesis that all of relevant reality is "spiritual." Nevertheless, this new understanding of the status of scientific concepts as symbolic has reduced the tension with other forms of knowing and so other forms of symbolism: artistic, intuitive, contemplative, and religious. On the older view that accepted empirical science as the sole cognitive avenue to reality, these latter were noncognitive, only "emotive," providing information only about our own subjective states—whatever, in a totally external, objective, and vacuous world, *those* might turn out to be! However, as religion has for some time relinquished its claim to know everything, so contemporary science is beginning to relinquish its claim to provide the sole mode of cognition and the sole reliable models of reality—and that will help us all when this is finally widely recognized and assumed.

Secondly, as we noted, the creative rise of science in modern history brought along with it, as one of its quite possibly unintended results, a new religious vision or new "myth" about human being in history: about the redemptive power of informed technology, the unreality of the older issues with which religion and philosophy had dealt, and so about the unlimited promise of the new world that was aborning. Science here tended to function as an instrument of redemption in history, as a religious reality making religious claims—as religion had once posed as an unquestioned authority in scientific, legal, and political matters. This role science has now largely eschewed; and as a result of this abdication, the pressing reality of our contemporary technological dilemmas, the common value and validity of other ways of knowing, of art, morals, and religion, can be more clearly seen even within a scientific culture. At one time, science seemed to make religion difficult if not impossible, not only because religion had claimed the competence of science in matters of fact, but also because science had usurped the role of religion as the sole effective redemptive force in history. Now that both have largely ceased to make these claims, their ancient warfare may be said to have ceased—at least for the moment.

Separation, however, is not the final word between these two, nor should it be. As we have noted, communal life is *one* and forms a whole with cognitive and technical tasks, artistic, moral, and legal tasks, and religious affirmations, obligations, and requirements. The religious should not replace, rule, govern, nor direct the others from the outside; nor should any of the others seek to replace religion. Rather do all these elements in the foreground of culture, the special disciplines and professions, depend in the end on some participating apprehension and appropriation of reality, truth, and the good, and on some symbolic structuring of that vision. From this religious center, the cognitive, normative, and artistic life of the society flow; and from this center its personal vocations and political forms of life receive their meaning, their goals, and their enlivening hopes. If this be the real role of religion and of religious faith, then religion in this wide sense is essential to any culture's life, even though that culture be scientific. In fact, as even the example of Nazi Germany showed, the religious and the mythical, rites and unconditioned obligations, will be there in *any* case in every culture, in creative *or* demonic form, providing the ultimate principles guiding that culture's scientific, technical, and political life. What is important, therefore, is not so much that the religious be "possible"—for it surely will be—but rather that the religious faith and its relation to cultural life be of the right sort.

This leads to our final question: not so much what kind of religious faith is possible—for apparently the most bizarre forms are possible; rather, in a scientific culture, which kind of faith is the *most creative*—a normative question. In fact, several requirements for a creative form of faith have appeared out of our discussion. And it is, I might remark, because of the character of these requirements and because of the relevance of the Christian faith to them, that I personally have found that faith most adequate to the needs of a scientific culture.

First of all, a creative faith in a scientific age must be able to comprehend, shape, and deal with *all* of those basic religious issues and their corresponding religious dilemmas which a scientific culture produces: the ethical/social questions of power and of justice, the metaphysical/ religious questions of the direction and meaning of history and nature, and the inward, religious questions of our estrangement or sin and of our creaturely mortality. Some forms of faith, and most ideologies, ignore one or another of these issues, and thus are less adequate. Secondly, a creative faith must undergird and not constrict, repress, or oppress our autonomous intellect, our autonomous decisions, our own artistic creativity and our legal/political structures and actions; it must be *theonomous* and not *heteronomous*. A scientific culture has rightly learned to prize independence of thought and speech; the freedom to criticize old formulations and inherited goals; the freedom to experiment with new hypotheses, new methods, new values; and the willingness to appreciate and to learn from viewpoints that differ fundamentally from our own. As we have seen, a union of science with religion will take place in *any* case, possibly in nationalistic, racist, ideological, and thus in intolerant and oppressive form. If, therefore, the religious is creatively and not destructively to unite with science, it must in so doing preserve and strengthen the humanistic values, as well as the purely "religious" values, of a scientific culture and not oppress or reject them.

Finally, a religious faith that can provide the illumination, the guidance, and the grace to deal with our strange human waywardness and orneriness must be realistic enough to recognize and admit the ambiguity of even our highest forms of intellectual creativity, the bondage of even the most extravagant forms of freedom, the driving self-interest of even our idealism. Thus, it must be able to be critical of even—perhaps especially—our highest cultural and spiritual achievements, conscious of the demonic potentialities of each of them, and capable of admitting those potentialities; and it must offer a grace that can transmute these demonic potentialities into actions genuinely creative of higher community. Thus, to grapple with both our finitude and our estrangement, it must point us beyond ourselves to the transcendent, "for except the Lord build the house, they labor in vain that build it" (Psalm 127).

The SACRED
and CULTURAL
PLURALISM

9

THE MYSTERY OF
BEING AND NONBEING

The encounter and slow interpenetration of the spirituality of the West and that of the East constitutes the major intellectual and religious event of our era. Its results in the Orient have for a century been spread before us in every facet of their thought and life. Its results on ourselves are largely still to come, but, like spring, they are bound in the end to make themselves known, and their signs are therefore of vast importance. On a somewhat lesser scale—to put it mildly—my own encounter with the East represents the major event in my own recent existence and thought, again an encounter in depth that is still pending, but which, like its larger counterpart, will be—for me at least if not for world history—of vast significance. I have, therefore, been tempted to address an aspect of this issue: preliminary ruminations on the effects of such an encounter.

I shall not speak so much of Buddhism, for there my words would neither interest nor inform. Rather I shall speak of the effects of an encounter with Buddhism on my own perceptions of my own tradition. New presuppositions and so new questions—and for a Chicagoan Buddhism is loaded with both!—have shed for me a quite different light on old issues and cherished points of view. Creative elements in our own heritage, long covered over and yet suddenly relevant to our new situation, are thereby uncovered; demonic aspects of our tradition, long thought relatively innocent, are revealed in their true light. This was vividly the experience of the East when the material, intellectual, moral, and religious power of the Christian West burst upon it; it is now *our*

123

experience. And long before we succeed in understanding them, we shall be deeply rethinking and reshaping our own tradition because of them.

The early church saw this point with regard to the Greeks, and all Christian thinkers reflected—though only a few welcomed—what they called "the covenant with the Greeks" that justified this interpenetration. For one who believes in universal as well as particular providence— and who has studied subsequent theology!—it is hard to limit to Hellenic culture alone the "covenants" that providence has apparently made as bases for our interpretation of God and his works. It seems to me evident that much as did Hellenism in an earlier age, so the modern heritage in the West has successively revealed creative aspects of our tradition ignored or unnoticed before, and uncovered as well mortal flaws in the Christian inheritance that had been given to us. In a similar way—and this is my thesis—in our day the "covenant with Buddhism" gives promise to serve the same purpose for us now as the covenant with the West, both Hellenic and modern, has in recent centuries done for us and in recent decades for them. For there is hardly a modern Buddhist thinker who will not freely acknowledge that he has learned new ways to interpret his own tradition from Western life, philosophy, and theology. It is, therefore, the new perspectives that Buddhism opens up on our own Christian tradition that I wish to discuss.

In the first sentence to an article on Paul Tillich's thought, the Zen scholar and philosopher Masao Abe asked: "Why does Professor Tillich—and all of Western thought—choose being rather than nonbeing, life rather than death?" I must confess that this question blew my mind! It took me at least an hour to get to the next sentence. This was partly because it so dramatically outflanked, or "burrowed under," what to us have been the primordial or most fundamental questions in philosophical theology and rendered them clearly secondary. The first of these questions rather rudely pushed to secondary rank is whether actuality is not more properly characterized as becoming rather than being. As process philosophy has rightly urged, this is an important question; but it is by no means the *same* question as Abe's. For "becoming" in Western philosophy is not the same as "nothingness" in Buddhism. Becoming represents a different, a modified, and perhaps a more coherent interpretation of actuality, and so of what the category "being" had sought all along to talk about. Over against nothingness, being and becoming become one, descriptions of concrete actuality as the seat of value as of reality. Secondly, it burrowed under Heidegger's and Tillich's "primordial" ontological question: "Why is there being rather than nonbeing," and showed the latter to be radically secondary to this more fundamental question. "Come on now," asks Abe, "Why do you think there *is* being rather than nonbeing, as your question obviously presupposes, in asking *why* this is so!"

The question—*is* there being *or* nonbeing, or neither—is, let us admit, a much more interesting, dialectical, and fascinating question. While this deeper question concerning being or nothingness, life or death, is like the other in its own way unanswerable, it is unanswerable on a more fundamental and interesting level. As far as I can see, the only answers to be found strangely yet inexorably beg the question, that is, presuppose an answer already having been given. For example, one could answer with Heidegger and Tillich that I choose being over nonbeing because nonbeing is the negation of being and therefore presupposes it—which clearly already presupposes the ontological priority of being. Or, one could answer, I choose being and life rather than nonbeing and death because they are clearly superior. To be and so to be alive are, as all but the schizophrenic know, better than not to be or to be dead. Again, the choice has already been made. Finally, it is no real help to answer that "God himself chose being rather than nonbeing by identifying his name (I am who I am) and so his reality with the former and not with the latter." For then another question appears inexorably—since, as Sören Kierkegaard says, the dialectic of questioning can never stop (*Postscript,* 35)—"Why did God—who was surely aware of the Buddhist question—choose being rather than nonbeing in naming himself?" Apparently, every ontological, ethical, and religious judgment primordial in our cultural life stems from the position one takes on this issue. We seem here to have reached a "basement" question, one that supports and illuminates all else we have to say.

Since apparently we cannot answer why most of us in the West choose being rather than nonbeing, it may be helpful to pose for our reflection two further questions related to this primordial one. The first is: *do* we in fact so choose, and if so how much; is the Western tradition tipped *entirely* on the side of being? And, secondly, *ought* we so to choose? Are there not in fact hidden values and emphases of our own that are grounded and guarded more by a qualification—perhaps a radical one—of being by nonbeing instead of a complete undialectical affirmation of being? Possibly, the frank Buddhist dialectic—nothingness is neither being nor nonbeing but the ultimate transcendence of both and so finally the union of both—better represents our own deepest and reflectively most coherent interpretation of our gospel than does our traditional "being-centered" form.

As we proceed, we should keep in mind what we may call the solely negative use of negation in most of our Western speech, philosophy, and theology. Nonbeing may not directly name the devil for us, but it comes near to it—whether we speak of the dissolution of the self as the ultimate terror, of the *"threat* of nonbeing," or of *das Nichtige* as the final antagonist to God. To many others of us, the category of nonbeing represents mere linguistic nonsense; to still others, it connotes an unaccountable flight from all that has reality and value in our experience. It has met with equal disdain from the this-worldly naturalistic and religious liberals and from the otherworldly orthodox. For each of these Western positions—and there are few others—to be actual, is and alone represents value: actuality *is* value, said Alfred Whitehead, and eternal life *is* blessedness, echoed the orthodox.

The traditional critique of philosophies of becoming by the "perennial philosophy" is that there is not enough "being" in such philosophies. In turn, the standard process critique of philosophies of being is that the notion of pure being becomes so transcendent that it reduces the reality and value appropriate to concrete actuality. In effect, *both* philosophies are in their own ways seeking to express systematically the Western concentration on and affirmation of actuality as it is disclosed in our own being in our world, and in our life within that world—the naturalists emphasizing that actuality in the experienced here and now, the orthodox emphasizing actuality in its continuation in the hereafter. Now, our point is that both Buddhism *and* important elements in our own tradition provide warnings against that exclusively negative or derogatory use of negation. Possibly *neither* being nor nonbeing are ultimate terms, but dialectically related symbols each in its own way expressive of the mystery of ultimacy, of the self, and of its destiny. In any case, it is with these questions in mind that I wish to explore our tradition.

Perhaps the best place to begin is to inspect the present deep ambiguity of being in our own tradition—or, as we noted, the category of being-becoming in its variant forms, for all represent an undialectical affirmation of concrete actuality. First of all, it must be said that this category—that of the reality and value of concrete actuality, of being—has expressed and transmitted a positive evaluation of human and natural existence, and that it has, therefore, grounded the most creative aspects of the Western religious and cultural traditions. The denomination of the Western God as "Being" and so the creator of finite being, whatever its roots in Exodus, Genesis, or even Hellenism, was no accidental error, by no means a total misinterpretation of what our tradition wished to say. On the contrary, it represented motifs central to the essence of our religious tradition and to its creativity. It helped to establish our sense of the goodness of the natural world, of bodily life within that world, and most especially of individual and communal existence within history.

Most of the creative values of our cultural and religious life find their deepest roots here: the affirmation of value to the concrete individual, of worth to the creative freedom of which that individual is capable, the conviction that responsibility for others and love between individuals constitute the highest good, and that time holds a promise within its unfolding, a promise of meaning and significance that will uncover fully the latent value of actuality. As everyone knows, (or should know!) these affirmations characteristic of Western culture—affirmations that have transformed other cultures within the past century—have their roots in a number of biblical symbols: in creation, in incarnation, in the experience of grace, and in eschatology. My point is that the "choice of being rather than of nonbeing, of life rather than death" finds its grounds here in the sense of the *positive* relevance of the divine to our human and historical actuality. This sense of the reality and value of concrete actuality is what the category of "being" brought to expression. It has been, therefore, appropriate that in this tradition this category has been ascribed, in its perfect form, to the divine: the reality and value fragmentarily sensed here in ourselves and our world is perfectly illustrated in the God who founds, rules, and brings to fulfillment that self and world. (It is to express these points coherently, adequately, and in terms of our religious tradition that every single sentence I have written in theology has been devoted.) As noted, to call this category "becoming" does not change this basic affirmation at all, though it may formulate it more coherently. In either case, we are pointing to concrete actuality as the locus of known reality and experienced value and ascribing it to God as its source and end. Both a philosophy of being and of becoming are Hebraic and Western in this fundamental sense.

To our surprise, however, the recent past and the present have revealed an ambiguous, negative side to this traditional undialectical affirmation of being as the name of God and, analogically, as the expression of finitude generally and of man's existence. In earlier periods of our tradition, when the sense of the contingency and waywardness of our life—of its participation in non-being—was ever present and vivid, "being" was predicated preeminently of God, almost exclusively and unrestrictedly, one might say. Through the infinite as well as the compassionate being of God, the precariousness of our human life in time, in history, and in sin was muted, and a creative, meaningful life in "existence" became conceivable based on the divine power and grace; so, it can be argued, spoke the great theologians: Augustine, Aquinas, Luther, and Calvin. However, as we are all aware, a God constituted by unrestricted being tends—if not watched carefully!—to threaten the being, the autonomy, the creativity, and the meaning of all else in the universe. An actively omnipotent being, foreseeing and foreordaining all, can drain of their reality and value the world and the life of creatures. As a consequence, freedom, finite value, and authenticity must struggle against God rather than on God's basis. God becomes a heteronomous being, crushing rather than establishing the world, and the modern protests—of eighteenth-century rationalism and materialism, of nineteenth-century idealism, naturalism, and radicalism, of liberal theology, of existentialism; of Feuerbach, Marx, Nietzsche, Sartre, and Heidegger, of Russell, Whitehead, and Fromm—appear in defense of the value and reality of becoming, of the autonomous individual, and of human culture. Let me be clear: God is not, I believe, heteronomous— and such is my point; but obviously a notion of God as pure being, as pure actuality, as infinite activity, as omnipotent power, can easily become so. Even "being" can become an idolatrous name. And of all these protests against the God of being, that of the Buddhists is the most pervasive and profound. Nishida echoes Nietzsche's cry that if the divine is being, sheer being, then there is no room in a universe filled by this heteronomous reality for finite freedom and authenticity. But the Buddhists do not protest, as does the West, only in the name of finite becoming and of the power and meaning of their own selfhood. Rather, conscious of the mortal danger of precisely that Western affirmation, they protest as well in the name of the sacrality of nothingness, another and quite different name for the divine.

The transcendent, omnipotent, all-sovereign God of being slowly receded under these protests. The Western affirmation of being, however, did not. It was, as the history of Renaissance humanism and of its child (born in a wedlock with science), the slowly developing Enlightenment, show, shifted from the infinite to the finite, from God to man, from the divine self to the human self—as if first Hegel and then Feuerbach wrote the script (as the former perhaps belived he in fact did!). In philosophy and religious thought alike, the reality and value of the self—the cognitive self, the experiencing self, the deciding self, the self-affirming self—became central starting points, as in the social realms the political, the economic, and finally the social self provided the major motifs. It is no accident, I fear, that this religious, philosophical, and social celebration of the reality, value, and power of the finite self, either individual or national, paralleled the almost infinite expansion of the culture in which these ideas gestated. For the West concurrently produced a political, economic, and industrial expansion whose power was grounded spiritually in an unrestricted affirmation of the self and its destiny, and materially in an awesomely developing technology.

Ideologically, the imperial ego, now of Western man and not of God, found its spiritual legitimacy in the unequivocal affirmation of being, of the power, meaning, and destiny of finite being: of the world to conquer, of the achievement represented by technological power, of the virtue and even selflessness of imposed rule, of the divine destiny granted to those who have discovered the means to survive and to survive well. Not many among the Western supporters of either the absolute Western deity or the absolute Western *humanum* protested *this* heteronomy; protests were felt only by those colonial lands swept up by this flood tide of material and spiritual power and affirmation. It is small wonder, again, that Buddhist observers, with one canny eye on the unity (*we* say the contradiction!) of Western ideals and Western behavior, and another eye on their own anthropology of nonbeing, should identify the philosophical affirmation and the religious worship of *being* with the imperial ego that carried Western flags and Christian crosses to every corner of the globe.

Apparently, whenever being is affirmed undialectically, it is overaffirmed, if I may put it so. First, such direct affirmation can render God into a heteronomous demon; then, as God recedes and finite becoming is celebrated, it helps to change *humankind* into imperial demons. The final example is that, with God now all but eclipsed, finitude turns on itself. Or to put this point more precisely, through our own enlarged and affirmed material and spiritual power, we expand not only over our less powerful fellows but over the nature that surrounds and supports us. A goodly number of apologists for Christianity, myself included, have been hoisted uncomfortably on this self-made but sharp dialectic. For several decades, we proved to our own satisfaction (if not to that of our two or three secular listeners!) that Christianity, far from being the foe of humanism, science, and technology, constituted in fact one of their necessary, if hardly doting, parents. Our tradition had sired these fondlings—like many sires, to be sure, unintentionally!—through its desacralization of nature, through raising humanity made in the *imago Dei* far above a soulless nature, and through proffering to a feisty race the prospect of an intelligible, manipulable, and satisfying natural world as the object of their ambiguous desires and purposes.

Now, to our horror we have found that this virtuous, if unwilled, Christian grounding or begetting of science and technology has been revealed—like the virtues of Augustine's pagan worldings—to be but one massive vice, destructive, like all vices, of both nature and of ourselves and hardly something of which to boast, as one discovers quickly enough in Japan!

This is a strange dialectic revelatory of important issues between West and East. The creativity of this transnatural Christian humanism and historicism—of human being viewed as raised above nature to be the seat of value and of spirit, and so of nature as only the theater of human history—is well known. It is, as noted, responsible for those creative gifts that the West has offered to the East—as every Buddhist is aware. But it has also a demonic "underbelly," disclosing itself to us now through the technological might and its greedy use that that humanistic, historical culture has made possible. And though our Christian tradition has, even more than that of the Greeks, laid the spiritual foundations for this imperialism of human culture over nature, unquestionably the humanistic *spirit* and the scientific, technological, and industrial *power* generated by the non-Christian naturalism of modernity have increased that imperialism. Officially and intellectually, to be sure, modern naturalistic humanism has, so it claims, reduced humanity's estimate of itself and relocated our race back into the bosom of nature as "merely an animal." Nonetheless, the *Geist* that rules over and speaks through Western naturalism—capitalistic or socialist—is a *Geist* of a human superiority to a soulless nature, a demonic superiority, heedless, greedy, and infinitely concupiscent, expressing the desire of humankind to draw the whole world into itself (as Tillich put it); the user and conqueror of nature—or, expressed philosophically and more delicately, the one whose informed intelligence transforms a blind, natural process into the materials for human ends and purposes—as John Dewey would put it. The power of being in modern philosophy may be said to rest ontologically in nature; but in concrete existence that social power is located and reveals itself—as Dewey, Whitehead, and Heidegger agree—in and through humanity, in its intelligence and will, in its freedom to manipulate and remake for its own ends the natural world and itself. Here, let us note, much existentialist and phenomenological disdain for the "objects" and "things" of the natural world is thoroughly in accord with the technological and industrial will to manipulate; the intellectual terms and the moral goals of these seemingly opposed phases of our culture are different, but their common spiritual alienation from nature is identical. That this undialectical emphasis on the human and its creativity, the most positive deposit of the traditional affirmation of being—first Christian, then humanist, then technological and industrial—should *itself* be revealed as a partial, and so a dangerous and destructive, untruth, or at least untrue enough to effect our alienation from nature, our despoliation of nature, and finally the loss of the human itself in a technological and consumer culture, is a rich irony indeed. To affirm ourselves and the world may in the end be a means of losing both. This wisdom, as old (let us note) as our own tradition, now seems to be verified in an unexpected and lethal way.

In any case, the intellectual tradition of the West, theological, philosophical, and social, and its accompanying modes of individual and communal behavior, seem to manifest deeply the ambiguity of being and now of its (somewhat antagonistic) child, becoming, insofar as both have represented an undialectical affirmation of concrete actuality as the locus of reality and value. And insofar as each of the West's theological traditions has associated that affirmation of reality and value with deity, the ambiguity has not been dissolved but increased. If the category of being means, as it surely does to the Buddhist world—and I have sought here to rephrase and to strip of their diplomatic coating their central arguments—not merely the transcendent, heteronomous deity of an older tradition but also the world and self-affirming, and so the world-conquering and finally world-destroying, imperial ego of the West, then one wonders if the Lord—whatever she/he may in truth be—felt "flattered" by having been for all these centuries dutifully and obediently named "being"! Did that central analogy of orthodoxy, characteristic of all of our major traditions, really succeed only in comparing her/him to the imperial, dominant ego for which we all yearned? Was it therefore in part only an infinitely subtle way of flattering, disguising, and legitimating the expansive self? To distinguish the self and God as "subjects" from the natural world as "objects"—note *our* major question in anthropology and theology—is not only to guard humanistic and theological values. It is apparently, and from a Buddhist perspective, also to establish an ideology for an industrial and commercial culture intent on the conquest of others and of nature. In short, to describe the ultimacy represented by God undialectically as being rather than nonbeing— whether we speak of deity as the "power of being," as the "principle of concretion," or as "necessary being"—may be to harden and to sanctify that ideology. Here are the deeper questions to us hovering behind Abe's initial query—a query which at its first appearance seemed startling, esoteric, and possibly inane—why do Professor Tillich and the tradition of the West choose being rather than nonbeing, life rather than death?

Such questions are painful and upsetting because they challenge the things we value most and of which we are most sure—that is, most proud! That the world affirmation expressed in the category of being or actuality, and in the identification of God with both, may be the principle of world destruction is a new note to us. It suddenly gives relevance, meaning, and coherence to the heretofore meaningless categories of nothingness and of nonbeing as applied to ultimacy, and through that to nature and the self. In these negations may be represented, so to speak, final safeguards against the imperial ego and its ideological legitimators, categorial ways by which the expanding self is checked, quieted, reduced, and finally dissolved rather than further unleashed and empowered. Sitting in Zazen and seeking to bring repose to the body and to empty the mind; gazing quietly at the infinite transcendence, coolness, and peace of Buddhist statuary; or pondering the sacrality, eternity, and peace of nothingness are thus merely variant ways—and there are others—of the same self-transcending process, as deeply antithetical—or so it seems at first—to a Christian harkening to proclamation of the gospel of life, or to theological reflecting on the being or becoming of God in creation and history, as is possible. So it seems at first, and so possibly it is. Nevertheless, what I would like now to explore briefly are those elements of nothingness that abound in our own tradition, in that very gospel of life and in that theological tradition concerned with God and history. These are, to be sure, elements often ignored, covered over, or reinterpreted—but nonetheless surprisingly omnipresent, central, and significant.

Perhaps the main reason we are so little aware of these elements or "rumors" of nonbeing is that they are rarely taken, as in Buddhism, as names or symbols of essential deity and essential selfhood. Negative predications have by us been construed as roundabout expressions of ways God has *more* being than do contingent, temporal, finite beings; and, correspondingly, the central negative elements within divine revelation, or implied by it, have been construed as temporal, instrumental, "economic" negations of God's full being and the being of the self. Neither the philosophical nor the religious negations have been taken as ways the divine reveals itself as a nothingness transcendent to being as we know it and experience it in ourselves. In this way, an encounter with Buddhism—and with our own tragic history—may not only lead us to look anew at the negating elements of our own tradition; it may also help us to interpret that tradition in the light of these same negating elements—to use them as central hermeneutical principles—as the Buddhists have been forced to reinterpret their tradition because of their encounter with us. It is not unfair to say in the latter connection that under the impact of the Western emphasis on being, on world and self-affirmation, and on what at its best had been our emphasis on freedom, authenticity, and real relations with others, a good deal more "being" has sneaked its way into modern Buddhist philosophy—at least in Japan. This, I may add, is by no means inappropriate at a time when Buddhism may be forced to think out a positive communal ethic, a new view of nature, and a religious interpretation of history, all of which were formerly borne in that culture by Confucianism and Shintoism and yet all of them opened up anew and in crisis form by the political, economic, and technological modernization of Japan.

I would like to suggest that when one scans our Christian tradition with these disturbing questions in mind, one uncovers there at the profoundest level a dialectic of being and of nonbeing, a dialectic that cannot be brushed aside, explained away, or *aufgehoben* into direct statement—lest it have the results we have shown. As I have argued, this polarity represents a far more significant polarity than our local Chicago polarity of being and becoming; and it is, I will argue, inclusive of all the essential elements of the gospel as well as of our talk about God: that is to say, of incarnation, atonement, and redemption as well as of creation and providence. This dialectic may, at some risk, be summarized as follows: being *is* a manifestation of the divine. That manifestation, however, is—I would like to suggest—more dialectical than analogical, a dialectic of both being and non-being, negative as well as positive, nothingness as well as being—and the creative aspects of each (of nothingness and of being) are intrinsically dependent upon this polar relation. This dialectic qualifies all we know of the divine activity and so all we know of deity: it appears in the realms of creation and of providence; it becomes clearer in each case of revelation; it reaches its climax in the kenosis of incarnation and atonement; and it represents the central criteriological principle governing every interpretation of resurrection and eschatology. This principle—perhaps most clearly stated by Kierkegaard—that the divine manifests itself only in a dialectic of negation (*Postscript* 218–20, 386–99, 407–12, 424, 467–74), transcends even his interpretation of it, I believe. For it means not only that negation, hiddenness, incognito, and what Kierkegaard called humiliation—aspects surely of nonbeing—qualify eternity *in* time, God *manifest,* God *as* man. Rather the negation, nothingness—and this is my main point—provides symbolic clues to the essential, not only the "economic," character of the divine ultimacy, and subsequently it opens up the character of our own essential being as selves. To predicate being and/or concrete actuality to God exclusively or univocally, nondialectically—as necessary being, perfect being, the fullness of being—is to raise, nay, even to project, the urge of the contingent to be, to survive, even to expand; to project this urge to the level of deity is a category mistake, if undialectical, that most of the gospel is intent on challenging.

If our tradition is interpreted aright, even being itself, or pure being, does not represent the central or determinative direct statement about God. Instead, it represents one polar symbol taken legitimately from our experience of finitude and our gratitude for our existence, and responsibility for it, and so applicable, but applicable only dialectically in correlation with nonbeing, to the mystery of God—since also our own being can only be affirmed in dialectical correlation with the affirmation of our nonbeing. God is being qualified dialectically and yet essentially by nonbeing, and so the divine mystery transcends the categories of both being and nonbeing. It is in this dialectical pattern, I shall argue, that God is manifested in all activity; and it is on this pattern alone that the self can find itself . . . by losing itself.

The principle that the divine manifests itself as a dialectical unity of being and nonbeing, being and nothingness, runs throughout the major symbols of our tradition. Creation, as we know, has always been the launching pad for the analogical but undialectical ascription of infinite being, necessary being, the perfection of being to the divine. We note, moreover, that the Buddhists, in ascribing to Nothingness the origin and source of whatever is and is not, have a difficult time avoiding the category of being. In this connection, as my friend Professor Takeuchi on a long walk in an exquisite temple garden admitted, Nothingness must be qualified by being. Nevertheless, as Kierkegaard notes in his *Journals* (Dru 180), in creating autonomous and free creatures, God reveals, to be sure, his omnipotence (only omnipotence, he argues, can create a being that's free), and yet God also just as unmistakably "steps back," qualifies his own infinite being with nothingness, and thus alone does God give room for that freedom which infinite being creates. Paradoxically, nonbeing in the divine ground of all must be there if finite being is to be there at all. Thus, the classical basis for the ascription, by analogy from finite being, of unrestricted being to God, namely, the experience of the sacral reality, potency, and value of finite being, is also the basis for the dialectical ascription of nonbeing to God.

Correspondingly, and on an even deeper level of manifestation, the symbol of providence also entails the dialectic of being and nonbeing. This entailment has been sensed throughout the tradition, and manifest in the intense philosophical and theological difficulties—not to say impossibilities!—of this symbol. For the symbol of providence points to and thematizes in language the divine activity in time and amid contingency, the paradoxes of eternity amid temporality, of absoluteness amid relativity—in difficult conceptions, to say the least, for either the Catholic metaphysics of pure being or pure actuality, or the Reformation conception of an eternal, absolute, and foreordaining divine majesty. As Whitehead and Tillich both recognized, for God to be related to a changing world, to be dynamically active in cosmos, history, or individual existence, God must be conceived in terms of becoming as well as being, of potentiality as well as actuality, and so—as both asserted—as the principle of future possibility as well as of past actuality. Thus, God as creative providence unites dialectically the power of being originative of each present, and the relative nothingness of possibility—lest the reality of the present as the locus of finite decision and so of finite selfhood be denied. A necessitated world—a world with no possibility and no future, a world "full of being"—smothers the reality as well as the value of the being of finite spirit. (B. F. Skinner is an odd end to the affirmation of the power and reality of the finite mind with which his scientific tradition began!) Again, for finite being to be there, the nonbeing of potentiality must be there as well, and must, if the potentiality be real, be shared in by the divine as creative providence. The divine in time, as in the original positing of free creatures or entities, manifests itself as sharing in becoming and thus as uniting dialectically being and nonbeing.

This theme—the nothingness that is also characteristic of God—reaches its climax in Christian discourse in the events of Jesus' "birth," of his life, and of his death, in the symbols of the incarnation and the atonement. In these events, we affirm, the divine manifests itself—and that, let us note, is precisely what the tradition has said of these events, namely, that here uniquely and unequivocally the essential character of the divine is manifested. And, more importantly, the divine manifests itself here by means of all those categories precisely disclosive of the participation of our being in nothingness; namely, finitude, weakness, vulnerability, suffering, and death. The tradition has, as we know, despite its methodological pressures, been leery of ascribing these categories, expressive, so to speak, of the finitude of finitude, to God. For this reason, we may suggest, it has insisted on locating the mystery in the wrong place, namely, in the relation of God as absolute being to the weakness and death of the incarnate one. Perhaps the truth is that vulnerability, suffering, contingency, and death—nonbeing in all its terrors for us as a sacral nothingness—are characteristics of deity, shared in by deity and so themselves revelatory of the sacral nothingness of deity. The divine *being* can seemingly only create and sustain finite being by continually negating itself, by uniting being and nothingness in its own self. Correspondingly, and on a deeper and more significant level, the divine *love* can only manifest itself effectively in the mode of the negation not only of being but of becoming as well: by weakness, suffering, and death. To redeem our being, the divine must negate its own. And this, we say, is expressive of the inmost nature of God, whose being—and nonbeing—is love. The incognito of God in weakness—made familiar by kenotic and Kierkegaardian christologies—may not be so much of an incognito, a "hiding" of God, as a manifestation of the final mystery of the divine love and the divine being.

This mystery of the divine negativity may, for a world striving to continue in its being and even beyond its being, be fully as much of an "offense" and a stumbling block as is the traditional paradox of absolute being appearing as suffering contingency. In the incarnation, the presence of nonbeing reached almost polar parity with the presence of being;

on the cross, the balance shifted markedly towards nonbeing. If we believe these events to represent the determinative symbolic clues to the mystery of deity in itself, then surely this dialectic should be central to our understanding of and our speech about the divine nature.

Finally, it is patently clear that the Christian view of the self, as fallen and yet as redeemed, involves in a form parallel to the incarnation and atonement this deep and polar dialectic of being and of nothingness. When the self simply wills to be, "to be" in the direct, literal form of continuing securely and successfully to live and to live well, it cannot and does not will itself; it loses itself and becomes, as Kierkegaard points out, either a defiant imperial self or a lost nonentity. It can will to be itself only when dialectically it is willing to will its own insecurity, insignificance, even its death. Only when it is capable of resignation and suffering, of final nothingness, can its *true* being appear: its being in nature, its being with itself, its relatedness in love to others, in sum, its reality, authenticity, and its joy. It lives when it is willing to die, and so when it dies daily—as the patterns of the incarnation and atonement specified. On the one hand, to live directly as the natural man or woman—since we *are* in estrangement from ourselves—is to destroy self and other life; and, as our history witnesses, even to appropriate redemption directly: to claim that we have grace and so are redeemed, is on a further level to threaten life and to lose this redemption. On the other hand, to negate and seek to dissolve the self directly (the temptation of Buddhism) is not only to fail to lose the self but to court moral irresponsibility for our neighbors, for our natural world, and in the end to be irresponsible for the future of both. A dialectical unity of being and of nonbeing, of self-affirmation and of self-negation—sought but only elusively experienced in both the Buddhist and the Christian traditions—seems alone to promise love and peace, genuine freedom, genuine integrity, and genuine community.

There is much more that needs to be thought and so much more that needs to be said before these themes can become in any way appropriate to our traditional sources for theology, or adequate and coherent in uncovering the puzzles latent in our common, everyday experience of our being (and, I should now add, of our nonbeing!).

This has been, as my title indicated, an experimental project, an effort to look at ourselves and our tradition from the perspective of Buddhism, armed with the sharp questions raised within that perspective. Its aim is to refashion our tradition—as we have already done in relation to the Hellenic, the medieval, and the modern cultural worlds—in the light of that covenant with the East. As in the last century Buddhism has experienced itself as both forced to reinterpret itself and as willingly aspiring so to do—in the light of the modern West and of Christianity—so in the unified but extremely precarious world that is coming, we find ourselves facing the same tasks and the same opportunity. Most strangely of all, it may be that precisely because of the destructive power of the technological West, the questions that Buddhism offers will provide, as Tillich might put it, the new "situation" in which our gospel must be interpreted and through which it may become relevant and true for us again.

10

REVELATION AND AN
ANCIENT CIVILIZATION*

Our question concerns the relation of Christianity, or of Christian faith, to the powerful, promising, and attractive reality of China. This question is usually posed as the question of "mission," of bringing or of not bringing *our* gospel, *our* religion, *our* church to the Chinese. Such a posing of the question—with, let me admit, immense backing from both Bible and tradition—is, I shall suggest, historically and theologically misleading or almost fatally tempting. Its implications are that *our* religion in its present forms is transcultural, that it can and should therefore be exported as is, unchanged and untransformed. As a result, the question that is then put is: in what ways do *their* culture and their religious life need *our* religion and so *our* church? Already latent here, I suggest, are the seeds of the imperialism—and the ultimate ineffectiveness (for in spiritual matters the two are opposite sides of the same coin)—of recent Christian invasions of China.

In the place of this model of "mission," I would like to propose the model of "covenant." By covenant in this context I mean the patristic concept of the "covenant with the Greeks" through which the Fathers—or some of the more liberal of them—legitimated the synthesis of Hellenistic culture and of the gospel, out of which synthesis what we now call Christianity arose. Here, therefore, we are speaking of *our* history

---

*This paper was written before the death of Mao Zedong and so while "Maoism" still represented the powerful center of Chinese cultural existence.

and of the formation of *our* religion—so immediately everything is much less imperialistic and utterly different! This is, I say, a more helpful and accurate model with which to ponder the subject of the relation of Christianity to the old and to the new China.

The Catholic religion, and so of course ultimately Protestantism too, resulted from the movement of an apocalyptic branch of Hebraic religion into the new and alien world of late Hellenism. This was a world replete with social, political, and ethical norms and goals strange to those of the earliest Christian communities, a world reflectively structured by alien philosophical categories and permeated with a religious orientation utterly different from their own. Out of a slow, deep, and essential interpenetration of these two realities arose our Christian religion: an interpenetration in the areas of rite, of symbol, of ethical obligations, of forms of church organization, and finally of categories and concepts of reflective thought. Hellenistic culture was transformed in part—unfortunately only in part!—by the Christian leaven. In turn, Christianity—orthodox, creedal, episcopal, sacramental, "Catholic" Christianity—was expressed, made real, and existed within forms and categories of the Hellenistic world. To be sure, heresy appeared when the religious dimensions of Hellenistic life quite overcame the affirmations of the gospel. No historian, however, can deny that the orthodoxy that combatted and conquered heresy, and the creeds that sealed the victory, were themselve saturated with the categories of Hellenistic culture and permeated with the characteristics and aims of Hellenistic religion. This synthesis, pace Harnack, was immensely creative, as well as being inevitable. Catholics had better think this because traditional Catholicism is the result of precisely this interpenetration! It expressed and uncovered elements in the gospel essential to its full witness and its life; and it was surely in part this Hellenistic component that made it possible for the gospel to be a basic formative factor, as it was, of medieval culture and of subsequent Western civilization.

One other "covenant" or synthesis might be mentioned: the covenant with the modern West. Here again the cultural life of the modern world—its science, its history, its psychology, its political, economic, and social norms and goals, its moral and human self-understanding, its sense of time, history, and human destiny—have impinged as both a lure and a threat on the older synthesis with Hellenism. This *is* the problem of aggiornamento; and the present tensions within the Catholic church are tensions between an old, established covenant with Hellenism

and a new promised one with modernity. Liberal and postliberal Protestantism sought for two hundred years to establish a creative covenant
with the modern Renaissance and Enlightenment; Catholicism is finally
seeking, as, so to speak, a creative yet painful necessity, to do so as
well. This is a necessity because, as Karl Rahner says, only a *modern*
form of Christianity can speak to or be believed by a modern man; and,
as many of us have argued, a theology not in touch with our own "secular," daily existence is empty, void of meaning, and void of use. Think
what the implications of these points, which we here take for granted,
are for "missions." Such a synthesis has been creative because much of
what we most treasure and defend in modern Christianity has arisen
from this synthesis: its acceptance of pluralism, its tolerance, its emphasis on autonomy, its awareness that all dogmas and forms of religion are
historically relative, its drive to transform the world in the name of
justice and of love. As Hellenism once did, modern life has in its synthesis with Christianity uncovered and emphasized invaluable elements
of the gospel latent and even denied before. We cannot repudiate this
paradigm of the covenant and be ourselves as contemporary Christians.
We know in ourselves and in those we respect that a living Christianity
always appears of necessity in the form of a "covenant" with the cultural
life in which it seeks to live. The absence of such a covenant or synthesis
heralds either imperialism, the heteronomous imposition of an alien synthesis on the life of a new culture, or—and this is always the final
result—ineffectiveness, emptiness, and disappearance.

Here is a model in which there is creative life, an infinity of risks,
and a lack of imperialism. It is a model which the church—although
itself the result of this process—has consistently refused in relation to
other cultures. For this model implies other covenants, other syntheses,
and so the relativity of our own religious forms and concepts, of our
religion, of Christianity as a human religion. Forgetting how this synthesis arose, the church has sought to send other cultures this synthesis.
Or, put another, more theological way, it has sought to send *itself:* its
traditional language and concepts, its dogmas, doctrines, and theologies, its institutional structures and forms, its rites and liturgies, its
rules and norms. One cannot, as a modern Western Catholic, look at
any of these traditional forms of dogma, law, and polity and not feel
their Hellenic origin and what is to us their anachronistic character.
Every liberal Catholic is dedicated to bringing this whole religious corpus "up to date": in theology, liturgy, canon law, moral philosophy,

church structure. And yet we, who can hardly wait to bring this inherited corpus into the deepest union with the forms of the modern culture we share, are apt to feel an infinite risk when we contemplate, if we do, a synthesis with another cultural substance entirely. I need not press the irony in all of this. Do we think these forms save us, or that God cannot use the forms of others as he has used ours? Can he not establish a covenant with the Chinese as well as with pagan Hellenism and pagan modernity? Would not a Chinese Christian feel the same need of "aggiornamento" in terms of his or her culture as we feel in terms of ours—and one that goes not only into the peripheral realms of social policy but one that penetrates—as does ours—to the very heart: to rites, liturgy, theology, and moral understanding?

Three comments should be made before we turn directly to the issue before us. The first is that at least at the present there is hardly any prospect of the sort of synthesis that historically the covenant principle has represented, namely, a deep interpenetration of Christianity and Chinese culture. Christianity has little present prospect of entering in bulk the Chinese scene, and we hardly represent that culture. Only Hellenistic Christians could create the synthesis that became orthodoxy; only moderns can write contemporary Catholic theology. We are probably like early bedouin converts trying to foresee the forms of the fourth- and fifth-century creeds! Any present influences, moreover, seem to move in only one direction, our direction, the opposite one from movements in the past. We, to be sure, are deeply influenced by the present Chinese civilization; correspondingly, we are asking the question about our relation, as Western Christians, to that culture. They are scarcely asking that question! At present it is their theories and faith, their patterns of being human, that are impinging with power on us. Ironically, it is now we who look for a relation to that new, impinging cultural force that preserves what is "old" in us (Christianity, possibly some Western values). We are the Ch'ang Chih Tung and the K'ang Yeo Wei of our time! And our questions, let us be clear, may (like theirs) be really more about the shape of future Western culture and of our Christianity than about theirs!

Secondly, a further word should be said about imperialism. As I intimated, a religion can be imperialistic on two scores, interrelated but separable. First, when it accompanies, appeals to, and profits from the military, economic, and political power of its culture. This we have done enthusiastically: first with Constantine, and then across the globe as the church accepted security, wealth, prestige, honor, and glory from Caesar—and has in our day paid for it both in Caesar's coin and in the honor of our Lord's name. Second, a religion can be said to be imperialistic when the cultural forms which it invariably bears—for no religion but has a cultural expression—are made absolute and so are forced upon that new cultural situation. In the case of Christian missions, the Western cultural forms and institutions of Christianity—its life as a form of modern Western existence and as a form of religion—were regarded as identical with the gospel and the grace being mediated, by both Catholics and Protestants. Thus, instead of pointing beyond itself to its non-Western Lord and its transcendent God, Christianity pointed to itself as a Western religion—and sealed its own doom. These two forms of imperialism are avoidable if one is aware of them—and if we understand that God's covenants are wider than we think, as God's rain falls on all. The greatest present danger is that we may, in consciously rejecting both military and economic power and Western social, economic, and political culture, fail to see how Western our religion and our church are, and so seek again to move our religion and our church into union with the new China.

As is evident, the question of imperialism is not directly related to the question of the universality of a religious reality. In order to avoid imperialism, one does not need to repudiate the claim of a religion to universal relevance. Buddhism and Hinduism have appeared recently in our own midst certainly claiming such relevance; and two Japanese Buddhist philosophers have told me they expect America to provide the new home for Buddhism now that it is decrepit and dying in China and Japan! Despite all this, none of us would say, even if these efforts are successful, that this is "imperialism," although surely they bring with them much of their own cultural heritage from India and Japan. Why would we say this? First, because they do not depend on military, economic, political, or social power; and, secondly, because they seem quite open to the prospect of their own transformation into the terms of the life of America—and all of us would assume that that would happen. Their grasping power is solely in terms of their own genuine religious and ethical strength, and neither one insists on representing a Hinduism or a Buddhism untouched by modern Western culture. Universal religions—Buddhism, Christianity, liberal democracy, and Marxism—can and have functioned in that same way; they can proceed into new cultural situations without imperialism solely by means of the persuasive power and relevance of their message. On the other hand, each can and has proceeded into new situations imperialistically. Also, let us note that anyone who demotes Christianity from the status of a universal faith to a "culture religion," relevant only in its own cultural and historical situation, has already relinquished Christianity and adopted in its place some *other* universalist faith that is not regarded as "merely Western," possibly liberal democracy or Marxism. Each universal faith tends quite naturally to reduce the status and pretensions of its victims and its rivals. For each realizes, and rightly, that the essential structure of its own belief is radically compromised if its claims to universal relevance are rejected. The theological trick in all these matters—for cultural systems such as liberalism and Marxism as for explicit religions such as Buddhism and Christianity—is to preserve that sense of universal relevance and truth along with that clear sense of our own relativity that alone can dissolve imperialism and generate charity.

Finally, it is well to note that in any discussion of the interrelations of religion and culture—and so of covenants or syntheses—there are two different levels, so to speak, of a cultural whole with which any religion must make a synthesis—and, correspondingly, as we have noted, two different levels of a religion. This was true of Hellenism and of the modern West, and it is surely also true of contemporary China. There is first of all the level of cultural life as such: their science or forms of inquiry and of the truth; their social and political thought; the forms of art; social and personal norms, mores, goals, and so on. Secondly, there is the religious dimension, a dimension that appears in each cultural whole however "secular" it may regard itself to be, a dimension that is explicitly expressed in every organized religion. In an avowedly secular culture such as the modern West or Maoist China, the first level, the secular, cultural life as such, is all that is recognized. Most discussions of a synthesis of Maoism with Christianity that I have seen have only this secular level of the Chinese reality in mind when they project the form of a possible synthesis. If they regard Christianity as "merely Western," as exhaustively a cultural religion, then Maoism as a dynamic, living culture tends for them to replace as out of date the Western/ Christian synthesis. If they regard Christianity as a valid and universal faith, then this first level of Maoist cultural life—like the similar level of Hellenistic life—forms for them the lower, "this-wordly" basis in "nature" for a somewhat traditional synthesis in which Christianity provides the supernatural level, one dealing with the problem of life after death. Both of these views are, I think, too simple. They fail to distinguish the two different levels or dimensions of cultural life. Let us therefore make our own suggestions by discussing these two levels or dimensions in turn.

We shall, then, first seek to deal with the cultural level. How might Christian faith relate to the social, political, economic, and moral reality of present China? It is on this level that, to me, the clearest gains for Christianity and for our common future appear. The synthesis of Christianity with the modern West has had many creative results. But undoubtedly this covenant has brought with it an emphasis on the individual: his or her salvation in heaven; his or her conscience, autonomy, and freedom of spirit; his or her property and its rights—all of which, for better or for worse, have reconstructed Christianity from the medieval, feudal phenomenon it was into a democratic/bourgeois one. I do not wish by any means to repudiate this inheritance in its entirety. But it is, especially in its American variants, desperately weak, yes even mortally so, on the communal side. The embeddedness of the individual in and his or her responsibility to the community, the ineradicability and value of relationships and their obligations, the priority, therefore, of community obligations over obligations to the self, the absolute importance of the category of the "common good" as a balance to that of the person—all of these communal emphases are peculiarly oriental, as the Confucian tradition in both China and Japan witnesses. They reappear in modern, progressive, and creative form in Maoist thought and in the reality of the new life in China: in the principles of the Mass Line, of the polarity of elite and peasant, in the emphasis on the social origin and character of knowing and of theory, and in the identity of the substance of China with the whole *People* of China. The same creative rebalancing of forces appears in the subordination of technology to the people's needs, of the authority of the expert and the power of the pragmatic technician to the political and moral goals of society, and in the insistence that all theory be reinterpreted through praxis. These are not just the politization of life, the absolutization of an ideology, as many American observers maintain. They represent in principle the reintegration of elements of culture sundered in our own cultural experience and so in destructive conflict and dissolution: individual and community, rational organization and purposes, technology and human needs. In each of these cases, we in the West perceive the sundered and self-destructive reality; but our theories remain theories or hopes alone, separated as protests from the sundered reality. In China, the beginning of a reunion of these separated polarities appears as an actual and a powerful social reality—thanks both to its Confucian background and its present socialist emphases—one that seems to have effected not only a redirecting of public policy but of individual motivation and of obligation as well. As Western life created a new pluralistic society and a new individual autonomy—as well as new theories about each—so Chinese life, old and new together, seems to be creating a new society and a new individual oriented now towards the common good, and using Marxist theory and Western technology and rationalization only for those human purposes. If, as I believe, the central social and political crisis facing us at present requires a new synthesis of the tradition of individual freedom with the communal character of human existence, then it is surely modern China that will provide the inspiration and the guidance for the creation of that synthesis.

One further point: perhaps the deepest problem of the modern west, a problem this time shared equally by capitalist and socialist countries, is that of the relation of human creativity and culture to nature. Here, *none* of our extant domestic traditions are of much help, since for all of them the relatedness of human being to nature has been sundered by religious (biblical), humanistic, scientific, and technological forces that have formed the essential substance of all the aspects of our tradition. Correspondingly, Japan, whose traditions (Shinto and Buddhist) are on this issue healthier than ours, is now thoroughly technologized and (as we were) technologized with no higher principle of control. Consequently, Japan (so it seems to me), has little to offer except the nostalgic image of a past view of nature now quite beyond effective recovery. China, on the other hand, represents a powerful present reality that incarnates in actuality as well as in nostalgia and hope much of the traditional oriental sense of the unity of culture and nature in a harmony transcendent to and inclusive of both, refashioned into a new, radical rather than an old, hierarchical, and conservative Tao. Morever, this theoretical subordination of industry and technology to the principle of harmony has in China been enacted by means of a praxis that is explicitly interested in the control of industry and of technology in terms of the needs of community and of nature alike. Again, help on the deepest social issue of modern life—an issue in which the West, as with individualism, has revealed only its self-destructive ambiguity and at present lives only in hope of some new principle—seems to be present in theory, in praxis, and in ethos in contemporary China. There is, therefore, little question of the creative possibilities *for us* of a new covenant of Christian faith with the new cultural reality of China.

Every cultural whole, however, has a religious as well as a cultural dimension, a religious substance on the basis of which the cultural life maintains its unity, its power, and its meaning. If it be true, as I believe it is, that each culture expresses in all its cultural forms a particular grasping or vision of what is ultimately real, true, and valuable, and lives out in all aspects of its life that stance towards being and meaning, then it is *that* relation to and expression of being, truth, and value which forms the religious substance of that culture, be it Hellenistic, modern Western, or Maoist-Chinese. Such a view of culture as having a religious substance has been expressed in varying ways in nineteenth- and twentieth-century theoretical sociology and anthropology; it has been set in theological form by Paul Tillich, and in a poor-man's version by myself. Let us note that it represents an antagonistic position both to the exhaustively secular interpretation of culture of the Enlightenment and of Marxism, and to the natural-supernatural interpretation of culture of traditional Catholicism. For here the natural is permeated with the supernatural, while, as I have argued, the church is also expressive in all its religious forms of its cultural locus. Needless to say, this religious dimension of any culture's life infinitely complicates the relation of a religion such as Christianity to any given culture, be it Hellenistic, modern Western, or Maoist. For therewith the deeper problem arises, not only of the relation of Christian faith to the culture as such, but also its relation to the *religious* elements of that culture. It has historically been here especially that the real issues of a covenant or a synthesis have appeared.

Concerning this problem, the church has been clear in theory and ambivalent in practice. I have, for example, suggested that heresy is constituted by a capitulation to the religious idolatries of a culture, not by a use of its cultural forms. The Gnostic, Aryan and Manichean heresies plainly sought to set into Christian symbolic forms the religious visions of the Hellenistic world. They were countered (by Tertullian, Irenaeus, Athanasius, and Augustine) by the doctrinal affirmation of peculiarly Christian symbols expressing a non-Hellenistic religious orientation: ex nihilo, trinity, incarnation, resurrection of the body, etc. We should note, however, that none of these orthodox Fathers eschewed Hellenistic cultural categories in expressing what they felt to be orthodoxy and what certainly became orthodoxy. In order to effect their Christian opposition to Hellenistic religion, they used the categories of Hellenistic culture. The same point could be made about the so-called neo-orthodox in the modern synthesis, both Protestant (Barth, Bultmann, Niebuhr, and Tillich) and Catholic (Rahner and Lonergan). In order to express their "orthodox" theology meaningfully, they used modern categories of interpretation, and they deliberately sought *not* to combat the secular science, history, psychology, and so on of their time, i.e., they were *"neo."* However, in order to express a traditional theological position, each of them countered what he regarded as the false religious dimensions (not the cultural dimensions) of modern culture: its rampant individualism, its scientism, its principle of autonomous self-sufficiency, its belief in progress, and so on. The problem of the relation of Christian faith to the religious dimension of culture—when the liberal consciously accepts culture and even the orthodox must use cultural concepts—dominates the theological controversies of both the ancient and the modern church. It can hardly fail to be the most important issue in our problem: the relation of Christianity to either the old or the new China.

A synthesis is possible and necessary only when each side has something to offer, or, put another way, when each *alone* remains incom-indicated at length what the ancient and the present Chinese cultural reality may offer to the West and to Christianity: the strong moral and communal emphasis of Confucianism now refashioned in an egalitarian rather than a hierarchical manner, and oriented forward to new possibilities in history rather than backward to a sacred past. Here, both the Confucian tradition and the Marxist tradition have been transformed in relation to one another, a genuine covenant, a monument to Mao's genius. That the very different Western cultural emphasis on criticism, individual autonomy, and the value of the person has in the past and even in the present something to offer China, I do not doubt. But what does *Christianity* have to contribute? The answer that Christian faith proclaims a life after death and Maoism does not is both true and important. However, as noted, this answer merely sets Christianity on top, so to speak, of Maoist culture as its supernatural complement—as Christianity once provided the supernatural addendum to a Hellenistically interpreted nature. Such a view of synthesis composed of two relatively independent levels therefore represents precisely that synthesis which liberal Catholics are presently themselves struggling against in the West. And the reasons they are struggling against the older "orthodox" synthesis are: (1) it fails to appreciate the implications of the gospel for life in the world and so for any cultural gestalt, Western or Chinese, for any form of "nature"; (2) it fails to understand the religious dimensions of any culture and so its idolatrous possibilities; and (3) above all, it fails to contemplate the need to transform Christianity itself (to bring it "up to date") as it offers itself either to modern Western or to Chinese culture. Some other answer than merely that of the supernatural destiny of the soul—true as that is—must therefore be given. This question: what does Christianity have to contribute to the old and now the new reality of China, is probably a more important question for us than it is for the Chinese. If we have no answer to it, there is surely not much living content to our faith.

I shall try to suggest an answer in terms of three points. Obviously, all involve transcendence and our relation to it. Since Christianity is a religion and thus a mode of being, of acting, and of thinking in relation to the divine, the ultimate, the sacred, to God, what it has to offer is primarily a new form of that relation, a form which transforms but does not replace the various aspects of our cultural life in the world. Correspondingly, what the faith offers to Maoism is essentially a new shape to the religious dimension of Maoism—as Christianity sought to do with Hellenism and with Western modernity. Christianity does not replace the cultural life with which it is in covenant; it has no science, politics, sociology, or economics of its own to offer. Hopefully, by transforming the religious substance of the culture into one of its own shape (here is the relevance of the symbol of the Kingdom), it will transform and deepen all of these common aspects of culture into a more perfect realization of what they themselves intend. The biblical symbols and the communal faith that uses them to interpret experience provide, as Calvin said, the spectacles through which the divine power and meaning everywhere present in life—but hidden, dimly seen, and mistakenly worshipped—are disclosed, clarified, and made central in a new form. Through that new formation of the religious substance of communal life, a transformation of the culture as a whole may be effected. Our three points, then, seek to clarify how the Christian tradition might reshape the *religious* dimensions of Maoism into a truer and more creative form. Clearly my argument is circular: Maoism is incomplete on these three issues *only* when viewed from a Christian (or some other) perspective. From its *own* perspective it naturally needs no complementary principles, no grace beyond what it may itself provide. But this circularity is characteristic of all intercultural and interreligious discourse, and so, while it is well to recognize it, it should not deter us—for the question must be answered.

(1) That there is a religious dimension to Maoism is, I believe, undoubted. Like its sister, Western Marxism, and its distant cousin, the liberal view of Evolutionary Progress, Maoism presents a global viewpoint encompassing a view of reality as a whole and of its meaning, as a whole. This viewpoint is set in terms of a symbolic structure of remarkable depth and consistency. It is related to by individuals and the community as a whole through participatory faith, commitment, and obedience. It is a symbolic structure that stabilizes and shapes the institutions, the forms, and the values or norms of communal existence, that grounds the meanings of daily life, that structures the patterns of education, and that guides political action. Above all, in answering the deepest questions of the meaning of life, it relates human beings to the categories of the absolute and the sacred, and thus provides their fundamental principles of judgment and renewal, their grounds of confidence and hope, and the possibility of their creative existence. This is not to say that Maoism is *a* "religion"; it is only to say that like any fundamental cultural reality, it contains and lives from a religious substance and religious dimension. Further analysis of the character of Maoism in order to argue this point is impossible. I will take it as accepted and proceed from there.

Now, my first question is: what happens when this religious dimension is latent, nonexplicit, in fact denied—as is surely the case in any form of Marxism and clearly in present China? The denial does not remove the religious elements, the sense of the relation to the ultimate reality of process, to the meaning of history, to the promise of future fulfillment. Mao's genius is clearly evident in the way he has prevented that claim to absoluteness from settling onto and rendering uiltimate any *particular* plan or even theory, the elite vanguard, the proletariat or peasants, the party, the nation; there is here a sense of transcendence that is able, to a remarkable degree, to be critical, and permanently critical, of each of the polarities of socialism in process. However, this absolute element—which keeps the remainder relative—is there. Its preservation as a transcendent principle is crucial lest absoluteness settle again (as it did in Russia) on theory and on the party elite, or lest the religious dimension itself be entirely lost in a pragmatic expertise ultimately indistinguishable from its Western counterparts. Modern history is replete with creative cultural experiments whose religious dimensions were unheeded and suppressed. The meanings of such a culture can then disintegrate into superficial triviality; its norms and its call to justice can dissolve—and finally, in reaction, the absolute can return in primitive, parochial, demonic form. A cultural whole—and the more redemptive it is the more risky—that understands itself to be "religionless" is continually in danger of a profanization that loses its essential religious substance (a lack of its "Catholic substance"), or a self-absolutization that leads to the demonic (a lack of the prophetic or the "Protestant principle"). Both have occurred, and often in quick succession, in the West—and both still threaten us. China is by no means invulnerable to this possibility. Where the transcendent is not known and acknowledged, the creativity of a cultural substance is always in danger.

(2) The importance, nay the necessity, of the transformation of social institutions—of the structures of government, of property, of the relations of production, of the interrelations of social groups and classes—has been one of the major creative themes of modern world culture: democratic-bourgeois, socialist-Communist, occidental-African-oriental. It is the central theme of the forces of liberation everywhere and so of the theologies of liberation. This theme has historically been a creative result of the covenant of Christianity with the Enlightenment and with secular modernity. Its roots are, to be sure, in important part biblical. But it has been only in modern history that it has, for various reasons, become part of the self-interpretation of the church and of her understanding of her obligations. Its power, in the eighteenth- and nineteenth-century West and in twentiety-century Russia and the Third World, has been such as to raise the question whether there is really any *other* mode or dimension of "salvation" or "liberation" than the transformation of social institutions and an appropriate educative induction into them. Is liberation theology in this sense *all* of theology; is the message of the church and of the gospel *exhaustively* social, that is, political and economic, in its concerns? If so, then it is dubious how much Christianity has to offer Maoism—except possibly, as noted, an explicit appeal to the transcendent and a promise of life after death. Again, we can only touch on this issue. Nevertheless, like nineteenth-century liberals in relation to an inspiring and seemingly triumphant social democracy, we

must put the question: what does Christian faith, if it recognizes as creative and thus as its own obligation, this "demand" for the transformation of the institutions of society towards justice, have to say to a movement and a society centrally devoted to that transformation and clearly capable of creatively effecting it?

The answer, obviously itself dependent on a Christian view of our historical existence, is grounded in a distinction between our estrangement and its consequences in cultural life, between what has traditionally been called "sin" and what we might term "fate." The warped and unjust institutions of our common life: political, economic, social—of government, property, race, group, family, sexuality—can and do become a "fate" for those who live under their oppressive domination. Such institutions, incarnating injustice, can be inescapable for those born into them; they prevent and constrict our freedom to constitute ourselves and to share in the determination of our own destiny; they separate us from one another and from all meaning and worth in existence. As Marx said, they alienate us at the most fundamental level, destroying personal being and community alike. The suffering that arises from unjust social institutions is the clearest sign of the fallen character of history and, as modern theology has pointed out, of the ravages of sin in history. Since such institutional structures are the result of sin, since they create suffering and encourage further sin, they defy the will of God for human community and they are an offense to the Kingdom. On the basis of Scripture and of the implications of every basic Christian symbol, therefore, the eradication, insofar as it is possible, of "fate" in this sense is an ultimate obligation of the gospel. Liberation theology, and so the thrust of Maoism—as of the humanitarian movements of the eighteenth and nineteenth centuries—are essential aspects of theology. Correspondingly, both faith and theology are required to unite themselves with authentic political, economic, and social movements of liberation whenever the latter appear. True theology is inescapably political theology dedicated to social liberation.

On the other hand, warped, unjust, and oppressive institutions are not the *cause* but the *effects* of history's most fundamental problem. Consequently, political and economic liberation, however crucial, is not the sum total of the gospel. For these institutions in this distorted form do not appear from nowhere; their warped character is not itself uncaused, a simple "given," necessarily if inexplicably present in historical life. On the contrary, this warped character—as liberal democracy and Marxism knew well—is not necessarily an irremovable, unalterable aspect of historical life, else there be no point at all in the effort to eradicate or even to ameliorate it. Institutions arise, as warped, through the estrangement of our freedom. Human creativity has helped to create and fashion these institutions; the estrangement of our creativity accounts, therefore, for their inevitable bias, the element of distortion and injustice present in all of them. Thus, even the very creativity of each cultural whole is involved in the end in the ultimately oppressive character of its institutions—as the bourgeois democratic culture of the West and its most creative gift to the world, technology, clearly illustrate. How hopefully that culture once viewed the "innocent," "just," and unambiguous future that it dreamed it would create! How evident it is now that the very principles that formed that dream constitute the anatomy of our present problems, dilemmas, and suffering! Each creative moment of history's life rightly rejects and transforms the warped social destiny that it inherits; each believes that thereby it has rid history of its most fundamental problem, the root source of its evil—as liberal democracy and its Protestant equivalent viewed feudal aristocracy and authoritarianism and their Catholic justification. However creative, each in turn reenacts in its own forms our common human estrangement and produces for its children and for others its own fated destiny—warped institutions which call for transformation. A deep spiritual estrangement, as well as its consequent oppressive institutions, runs through history and itself needs healing. As freedom falls into sin in history, so the creative destiny we seek to bequeath to our children and to others itself falls into fate. The transformation of that social "fate" is a necessary task; but the redemption of the freedom that continually falls, and in falling recreates historical fate, calls for another dimension which our creative and even our revolutionary action in the world cannot provide.

This truth is seen implicitly by Mao when he speaks of the need for the transformation of the inner person as well as for the transformation of institutions, and when he recognizes the permanence of the contradictions of historical life and the continual reappearance (what is called the "redefinition") of both "proletariat" and "bourgeois" even in socialism. Social transformation deals with the consequences of estrangement and alienation, not with its deeper causes. Thus, estrangement and its consequences will reappear even when the given forms of fate in our time have been radically reduced. An explicit dealing with the problem of sin, as well as with fate, is essential—and this a social philosophy can never finally either promise or achieve. Our commitment to Christianity, as Augustine argued, is in the end based on the self-understanding that discovers our problem, the human problem, to be one of estrangement or sin, and that calls therefore for the answer of a grace beyond cultural possibilities—or the possibilities of our own intelligence and will. On this self-understanding, the relevance of Christian faith to every cultural situation is based.

(3) There is, as we noted, a remarkable sense in Maoism of both the mystery and the meaning of historical process, and the dialectical interrelation of mystery and meaning. For historical process is here viewed as a process of struggle between opposing but interdependent polarities, each dependent on the other but each critical of the other and balancing it. This struggle is seen as necessary in order to preserve justice and harmony; yet risk is also necessary in order to prevent their separation and destruction. Out of the relativity of the parts and the chaos of surface events, arises, therefore, a deeper meaning. Here is a picture of a creative process with religious depth, with an intrinsic principle of self-criticism, and with hidden but profound telos and meaning latent within it.

From the Christian perspective here enunciated, this view presents a profound interpretation of the providence of God as it works in history, a hidden purpose working through judgment and new possibilities to create deeper meaning. It is, however, intrinsic to that Christian perspective that an even deeper dialectic appears in the course of history, a dialectic symbolized not by providence either as judgment on the old or as promise of possibility to the new. Rather it is dialectic symbolized by the cross and the resurrection. For us, as we have seen, the dialectical process of creation, opposition, and struggle is at once a process of a human creativity enmeshed in sin or estrangement, and so is also a process qualified by judgment and grace. The transcendent is present in the process as the ground of creativity and of new possibility, of a dynamic surge through struggle into the new—as Mao recognizes. But the transcendent is also *over against* the process as the principle of judgment, of prophetic criticism of those who rule and even of those who revolt, a principle of judgment of *all* in order that *all* may be rescued. This dialectic, which is the heart of Christianity, can never be present unless the transcendent is recognized *as* transcendent, unless judgment on even the creative, the wise, and the good is made explicit, unless grace appears as powerlessness and suffering as well as victory, and life appears after and through death. The cross and the resurrection hover over the creative process as the sole principles of its continuing creativity. Unless even what is most creative knows its mortality and is willing to die, it can hardly live without destruction. Unless life arise in history continually out of the possibility and reality of death, it can hardly live. This Christian principle is dimly foreshadowed in the principle of dialectical opposition, and more clearly seen in the principles of continual revolution and the Mass Line. However, only as explicit, only as internalized, only as appropriated in and through the presence of repentance and grace can it be real and permanent. Only if the life of the human spirit dwells explicitly in humility, repentance, trust, and hope in the presence of the eternal can that life enact this final dialectic and be creative. The Christian symbols, centered on the cross and resurrection, do not "save us"; grace does. But they can create for us a self-understanding and an ultimate horizon within which we find ourselves *coram Deo,* in the presence of God, reconciled, reoriented, and reborn in an inward stance where presence and grace may be received. This gospel must be heard anew, both here and there.

The supreme irony of history—and the supreme illustration of history's need for this message—was that this gospel of judgment on all, even on us ourselves, that grace may be present in all, was proclaimed via gunboats, commercial goods, technology, and the self-affirming ego of the West, not to mention the power and authority of the triumphant church! It would be equally ironical if it were to appear once again, in a land now deeply devoted to the masses, in the guise of a new ecclesiastical invasion of the mainland, planned and enacted with all the devotion, resources, and ingenuity of the vast ecclesia. Only a community *itself* under judgment that grace may come to *it* can give *this* message to a China newly reborn in history out of near death. Only a mission that eschews it own power and glory—technological, military, Western, ecclesiastical—that receives a judgment on its own culture and religion, can communicate this message of judgment on and grace to the culture and religion of the new China. The church has too long proclaimed justice, reconciliation, repentance, love, and unity to the world, and quite forgotten to apply these stern requirements to its own life and even to its own mission. The word of God's judgment and grace must first be heard within, acknowledged and appropriated by ourselves, if we are to speak that word in the Spirit to others. If the church merely brings its own culture and its own religion, its Western forms and rites and its ecclesiastical might and power—even if, in *our* eyes, these proclaim the cross—it will rightly be rejected again. A mission that dies itself, that sacrifices what it is in the world—in culture, in religion, in theological formulations, and in ecclesiastical might—in favor of the transcendent to which it seeks to witness, can be heard—both in China and here. For that alone is the voice, and the commission, that comes to us from the cross and from beyond the tomb.

11

TOWARD A REDEFINITION OF UNIVERSAL SALVATION IN CHRIST

In attempting to discuss theologically the relation of the many religions to truth and salvation we are—let me say at the outset—embarked across what is an almost uncharted sea. Few have successfully sailed here; the risky reefs and also the safe deep waters are as yet unknown; there is no established tradition that can help us, nor dependable pilots who have been there. No longer can any twentieth-century theologian either assume that truth and salvation do *not* exist outside of Christ or assume that he can continue to avoid the issue as if it weren't there.

Partly to blame, or to thank, for the situation that raises this problem so sharply for us is the new but deep experience of the relativity, the vulnerability, even the partiality of our own Western culture and—in a quite new sense—of the religious traditions inherent in it. Heaven knows, this Western culture since the eighteenth century has sharply pointed out to all of us the relativity, vulnerability, and partiality of our religious traditions, Catholic, Protestant, Christian and Jewish. But now—and this has tilted the balance—Western capitalistic, individualistic, democratic, scientific, technological culture has revealed its own partiality, insufficiency, and possible mortality. Suddenly, therefore, the other religions appear before us with an undeniable new beauty and a disturbing new power, as clearly equal (if not superior!) in sophistication, depth, wisdom, and healing efficacy to our own. No longer, therefore, are they to be easily written off (however politely) because they have provided no grounds for those values of individuality, selfhood,

157

social development, science, technology, historical progress, and so on, values which we took to be obviously sacred and ultimate. Now we are by no means sure those aims and values are all that salvific! Other values—community, selflessnes, spiritual contemplation, meditative techniques, a love of nature—where *we* are weak and *they* strong have come suddenly to the fore. Thus, while few of us have experienced "conversion," still, we can hardly claim the clear superiority of religious doctrine, ethics, or practice, any more than of Western cultural forms and values, that we long took for granted. And if *that* superiority cannot be claimed, then to claim for ourselves an exclusive salvation seems to most of us to be less a claim essential to the saving gospel than the last bizarre holdout of a superiority we had hoped that that gospel might save us from!

Our problem, I am saying, does not arise from new theological theories, which might be refuted and forgotten. It arises from a new reality that encounters all of us in our time whether we will or no, the reality of powerful, healing spiritual forces embodied in these non-Christian traditions. This is a reality we can hardly deny and remain honest either to the evidence or to our own experience. Thus, it is a reality no theological theory can explain away; it is, therefore, one which our theology must accept and then understand even if it effects a new shape to our former understanding. I take it we all assume this point, and that that is the force of the title given to me: a *redefinition* of universal salvation in Christ.

Creative relations between religious faiths are more than those characterized simply by the aim at conversion and the negative judgment of error or worse. They involve genuine dialogue, that is, a two-way dialogue to which each contributes, in which each learns, and from the results of which each grows. The clear intellectual implication of such dialogue is the presence on *each* side of partiality and possible error on the one hand and of truth on the other; the clear ethical implication is the possibility of salvation within each. Thus arises the specific set of dilemmas enshrined in this title. How can there be salvation in Christ that is *not* universal salvation; but how can there be universal salvation—salvation within and through *other* religions—in Christ; and how can he remain *Christ*—ultimate, decisive, absolute—if there is salvation elsewhere as well? Do we not have to give up one or the other, *either* the category of universal salvation *or* the category of Christ, of a unique and decisive savior for all? One answer is, of course, to dispense entirely with the latter category and merely to say "Christians prefer Jesus." But then, unless we cheat or ground our theism in a very parochial Western philosophy, we are actually within a humanist horizon according to which all religions (however tolerant we may be personally) are *as religions* equally false because in a naturalistically interpreted world only an ethic patterned on his life and teaching can be "true." Such a horizon, being Western, naturalist, and humanist in character, has its own dialogical problems recognizing the truth and value of the religious elements of other religious positions instead of, as it is wont to do, regarding these elements as simply error.

One way to begin to unravel these dilemmas is to note and face squarely the paradox latent within the question of universal salvation itself. The paradox can be called the paradox of the *certainty* of a *universal* salvation. This is a paradox because, on the one hand, it assumes that we all know or believe on some ground or other that there is salvation and thus that the religious "knowledge" of salvation which we possess is insofar certain and absolute. Yet it also presumes that salvation is universal. But if so, then no one way to it can be absolute, and so all ways are relative. Strangely enough, on the one hand it seems to be impossible to *know* of universal salvation without some absolute principle of certainty, and yet on the other hand it seems impossible to have *universal* salvation once we adopt such an absolute principle. Let us now unpack this paradox and uncover its implications for our thought.

Let us note, first, that salvation, universal or not, and whatever we may mean by it, is by no means to be taken for granted as a "datum" or a simple "given" in experience; nor is certainty about it a part of common sense, a conclusion of science, or even a result of an intelligent look at ordinary experience. Rather, knowledge of the possibility of salvation, and so the very certainty with which we began, has arisen for each of us precisely through that particular and special means of knowing intrinsic and unique to each religious or communal tradition, that central point to which all fundamental appeals are made. In some traditions, this is a mode of special revelation on which the religion is founded; in others, it is a special level of consciousness or mode of knowing where ultimate certainty can be reached; in some it is a combination of the two.

The reason for this structure is obvious: *salvation* receives its meaning, as do other words, by contrast to a situation of disruption, alienation, lostness, and ignorance—and it is "ordinary experience ordinarily taken" that is so described. If we speak of salvation, therefore, we mean rescue *from* that common situation by some extraordinary and unique means, not just *any* old understanding of or dealing with that common situation. Let us also note that this sort of unique principle of rescue can be quite "secular": through psychoanalysis, through Marxist revolution, through scientific method and technology, as well as through some special religious means. In every case, however, in both the secular and the religious examples, the knowledge and the certainty of salvation are hitched to and dependent on the particular means by which that rescue is achieved. The knowledge of the possibility and reality of rescue comes only with the experience of rescue, and each presupposes an absolute standpoint. Whether we refer to the Buddhist, the Christian, the Marxist, or the Freudian hope of salvation, none can speak of salvation at all without presupposing the cognitive solidity and efficacy of its starting point and so the validity of the knowledge gained thereby. Thus, to relativize the special means to salvation of each is, it seems, inexorably to entail the relativization of the special knowledge enshrined in that means and that tradition, and so ipso facto to render dubious the certainty it possessed that salvation was possible at all. To put it in terms of the two specific traditions of Christianity and Buddhism: the savior who brings salvation is also he who brings knowledge and certainty of salvation; the level of consciousness at which salvation is achieved is also the level on which its possibility is known. If these means of knowledge are themselves relative and as improbable as they are probable, if not thoroughly dissolved away as a means of attaining certainty, then our certainty of salvation itself dissolves with them into mere improbability, uncertainty, or even sheer illusion. The question of universal salvation has then shifted into the question whether there be any salvation at all. Probably to answer that deeper question, we now must enter again into some special tradition and trust once more its particular promises.

It seems that in order seriously to raise the question of universal salvation, we must stand firmly *somewhere,* in some tradition where the real possibility of salvation is known and affirmed; be it through a revelation, a savior, a way of meditation, or, if that be our preference, through a particular philosophy which then takes its place as *our* unremovable point of certainty. It also seems implied that while it is not contradictory to include other traditions in a salvation that is promised and known through one, it is strangely contradictory to make relative and thus to dissolve the knowledge of salvation when it has been precisely through the means of those particular traditions that the question of salvation has been initiated and made possible in the first place. Some fixed and therefore quite particular starting point for each member of the dialogue is essential if a real conversation about salvation, or about the extent of religious truth, or about the extent of the divine love, or other central issues in religious dialogue, is to be possible. If those fixed points are relaxed, the issues themselves of salvation, of religious truth, of the divine love dissolve into thin air and a dialogue *among* religions disappears. In its place, we would now be involved in a dialogue *about* religions from a nonreligious standpoint and so conversing about their collective errors and illusions, including the illusions of salvation, of saviors, of higher levels of consciousness, and of the divine love.

In sum, when we seek to speak of the question of the universality of salvation, let us at the start recognize and acknowledge the logical as well as the existential necessity of a particular standpoint from which the question of salvation can be broached, be it Hindu, Buddhist, Islamic, Jewish, Christian, Marxist, general Western, or philosophical. For without those particular standpoints, there is no such question left. With regard to our initial doctrinal dilemma, this means, I take it, that the "redefinition" we are looking for does not mean, and cannot mean, that we dispense with an authoritative center both of knowledge and of grace, that is, in our tradition, with "Christ,"—or, if we make *that* shift, with an unremovable philosophical starting point—however we may interpret or describe our unremovable center. But, of course, having reached clarity on that point, all the problems we wished initially to address now crowd upon us again.

Granted, then, that we all stand somewhere in order to know of salvation and to hope to share in it, and that Christians acknowledge that center to be the Christ or Jesus as the Christ, the question arises, does this standpoint of ours—or any of the many other religious standpoints—represent the *exclusive* place where such knowledge and such hopes are possible? Are there other ways of knowing about salvation, and are there other ways or means of participating in it? It is, I would suggest, in relation to these two questions that a redefinition is called for and is possible. For clearly the mainline traditions of Christianity have denied both validity and efficacy to religious traditions other than our own—even if the salvation of some individuals in those traditions, through election, grace, or invincible ignorance, was admitted to be possible. Let us discuss each of these questions in turn: first, that about the possibility of a universal knowledge of salvation, and then that of a universal participation in it.

One answer to the question of the presence of truth in other traditions—what I shall call the mystical or pantheist answer—has rightly been considered superior to the traditional Christian answer to this question. Instead of seeing other faiths as representing sheer error or illusion, Hinduism and Buddhism have viewed them as possessing a goodly amount of positive truth, and thus able to take their legitimate place among the many and varied ways truly and yet relatively to speak of the Ultimate, and among the many legitimate paths to effective participation in salvation. For both of these mystical systems, there can be and have been many revelations, each appropriate to those who received them. Each one is more or less true according as it approximated a mystical, pantheist form; and each one, if followed to the end, will lead beyond itself to the same end point, namely, union with the transcendent that is beyond all speaking, beyond all doctrines and symbols, and beyond all particular revelations and saviors. We note, therefore, that despite this admirable acceptance of other "vehicles," by no means are all religions made *equally* relative, equally true or false, for then we would live in a world where there would be no chance of salvation at all. On the contrary, an unmovable standpoint or core of interpretation remains that is not relative and that becomes the hermeneutical principle for assessing the relative truth and efficacy of other faiths. The ultimate reality remains in the pantheistic sense "transcendent" as the necessary basis for the affirmation of a plurality of ways; the salvation all paths are leading to is a particular mode of salvation, namely, union beyond all speech and differentiation; and, finally, with a particular level of consciousness, an absolute knowledge on which all this is based is reached. Thus is the cognitive and theological core of these mystical traditions preserved as the very basis for their impressively tolerant attitudes towards other faiths. A particular standpoint on religious truth is maintained as the logical ground for the assertion of "truth" in other faiths, as the criterion for the more or less of that truth, and as the basis for an understanding of the salvation all seek. As I have argued above, it seems to me that no answer can either avoid this logical structure of absoluteness within relativity or do much better than this one.

Although it will inevitably be more complex, this same sort of resolution is, I think, possible in a religion of revelation such as Catholicism—and, of course, such as Judaism or Islam. The affirmation of a universal and active presence of God in and through creation, history, and personal experience, and a corresponding awareness—dim though it may be—of that presence is implied by almost all Christian symbols. The fact that religions are universally present in human culture points to this presence and this responding awareness—though it probably does not prove them. I would also add, with Paul Tillich's help, that the rise and flowering of cultural life signals as well a general revelation of the divine power and meaning; for each culture has a "religious substance," a vision of and participation in an unconditioned reality, truth, and value on which it lives and which represents its appropriation of and response to the divine presence. Such a concept of general revelation, as it has been called, is the theological basis, first (as the Fathers realized), for the recognition of the truth in and the values of cultural life (in their case Greek culture); and, second, it is the basis for recognition of the truth, value, and saving power resident in other religious traditions (which the Fathers did *not* acknowledge!).

Now, it appears to me unquestionable that not only is the creative and providential activity of God present and manifested throughout nature and history, but also the *redemptive* work of God that culminates (for us) in the Christ is universally present, as alienation and sin are universally present. This is the clear and unavoidable implication of the reality of redemptive force present in other religions. It is because of the presence of the redemptive work of God in and through all things that the possibility of salvation has been known throughout the religious traditions, and hope for it is there grounded. If a strong concept such as this of the universal creative and redemptive presence of the divine is developed, the truth within other religious traditions can be affirmed without contradiction.

Of course, as the logical situation requires and the mystical answer illustrates, a particular and *un*relative standpoint where some truth about salvation is known and acknowledged is required and must be maintained if the truth within other traditions is to be recognized and affirmed. For example, the fact that many if not most religions speak of the divine as in some manner loving indicates the well-nigh universal presence of knowledge, dim as it may be, of that truth. But that we *know* that God is love in the first place—and so that these other religions are in that regard "in the truth"—indicates the sort of *un*removable standpoint of certainty I am speaking of: the certainty through a particular revelation or mode of knowing that God is in fact love. Thus are the concepts of general and special revelation polar concepts, each relative to and dependent upon the other. As Friedrich Schleiermacher said, there is no religion that represents "religion in general," "natural religion," or merely "general revelation"; there are only particular traditions, each with its own founding center, its own special revelation or mode of knowing—and of course the structure includes philosophical as well as "religious" ways of knowing. On the basis of that center, it is then possible—as again the mystical answer indicated—to recognize, to define, and to affirm the truth that is present in other faiths.

I have, then, suggested that a Christian can welcome the presence of truth about reality and value (as we would say, about God) in other traditions, and even a truth that leads, as all truth does, to greater fulfillment and healing. The Christian can affirm this because of the universal presence and activity of God as creator, providential ruler, and redeemer in and through nature and human historical existence. Finally, the Christian knows there is such truth about the possibility of salvation, and, so to speak, its general structure and anatomy, because he or she participates in that truth through Jesus as the Christ and takes what is revealed there as the basis at once for his or her certainty of salvation and for his or her interpretation of its character.

Lest this suggested union of the absolute and the relative—patterned with thanks on the mystical answer—seem merely a souped-up version of the traditional exclusivist absolutism, let me add to it two concepts that have newly appeared in recent discussion. The first is the helpful distinction—original I believe with Karl Barth—between revelation and religion. In contradistinction to the older liberal tradition, which regarded Christianity as the absolute religion, and therefore qua religion—in its doctrines, liturgies, ethics, communal structures, techniques, and experiences—superior to other religions, Barth pointed out that as a religion in this sense Christianity is merely human, a human response, and so hardly better or worse than other religions. What, he said, is unique about it is that to which it witnesses, the grace that is present in memory and in faithful expectation, namely the Word or presence of God: the *event* of revelation. Thus, the "absolute" to which the Christian points and on which his or her certainty rests is not "our truth," which is relative, partial, and incomplete, and deeply compounded with a relative and dubious Western culture; rather it is that Word which our truth seeks, humanly, inadequately and parochially, to express.

This principle, which I believe has real ecumenical possibilities, can, strangely enough, be supplemented and even deepened by a not dissimilar one familiar to students of Tillich, namely, the principle that only that person or that community can become a genuine medium or symbol of the New Being which points continually beyond itself, its culture, its own religion (in Barth's sense), its "characteristic particularity" to the transcendent. Thus, patterned on its own center in Jesus as the Christ, who was precisely such a self-transcending medium or symbol, the Christian community can become a symbol of the divine insofar as it points beyond its relative cultural and religious forms, quite away from itself, and centers its concern not on itself but on the God to whom it witnesses. Only in this way can the particular become an opening to the universal, not by abstracting in *thought* from its particularity but by pointing in its existence and its witness to the divine that is the universal power, meaning, and principle of redemption. Whether this view is orthodox or not, this juxtaposition of the absolute and the relative, and the subordination of the latter to the redemptive power of the former, sounds like the two natures! Let us also note that the same dialectic of the relative and the absolute worked out before is now here applied *internally* to the starting point and center itself. Thus, all that remains specific and particular, and so exclusive, about that central point is acknowledged as relative, and only its transparency to the transcendent is made central and absolute.

Possibly, for a religion of revelation in history, this principle of self-transcending particularity may be equivalent to the final relativity of all symbols so admirably characteristic of Buddhism. The use of a similar dialectic characterized Wolfhart Pannenberg's ingenious if strange resolution of this problem: every religion, he says, is incomplete, pointing to a fulfillment in the future beyond itself. That religion which knows this and so interprets itself thus represents an absolute position in its very relativity.

One other element mitigating the sting of this absolute starting point is that we would, I take it, all agree with Tillich that the eternal message, the presence of the divine, is always received into a given cultural "situation," interpreted from and through that situation, and expressed in its terms. These situations vary in history: there is the Hellenistic situation, the feudal one, the Renaissance and early modern situations, and the Enlightenment and post-Enlightenment ones. Each one of these situations, let us note, fashions the message into its own recognizable form; and each one obscures some elements of the message and uncovers other elements (as, for example, the Hellenistic interpretation obscured the social implications of the Kingdom and the modern has uncovered them). Realizing this point, certain of the patristic theologians spoke of the "divine covenant with the Greeks," expressing thereby their confidence that the Logos had revealed itself through Greek culture, that is, through certain of its philosophical and ethical categories and some of its dominant symbols—though not through its forms of religion! Thus, since divine revelation itself had helped to create these categories, it was legitimate for theology to use the forms of that cultural situation, "pagan" as it was, as means for interpreting the gospel. Implicit in our own current theological and ethical use of contemporary philosophy, literary criticism, the sciences of various sorts, and psychological and social theory (for example, socialist social theory) to help in interpreting the gospel and its implications is the same confidence that modern culture (liberal *or* Marxist), like Hellenistic culture, has in significant part itself participated in "general revelation," so that its categories can become faithful vehicles or means of expressions of the gospel. We hold, in other words, to a "divine covenant with modernity" in order to do theology as we all do it.

Now the point is that it makes perhaps as much sense to affirm (on the basis of universal revelation) that there has been a covenant, say, with Buddhism, as to say there has been one with Hellenism or with modern Western culture. There is truth—truth about nature, ourselves, and ultimate reality—there, and truth which our own Christian interpretations, limited as they are to the categories of a developing Western culture, do not possess. As the situation of modernity has uncovered for us elements of the gospel unseen before, so the situation created by Buddhist, Hindu, or Islamic religion and culture—the questions they ask, the emphases they make, the answers they find—may uncover elements of the final truth—of Christ, if you will—unseen before through the spectacles of our limited tradition.

The experience of another faith, like a mirror shining new light into our own, has been (as they have told me) very vivid in the recent past for many Buddhists in their encounter with Christianity. For example, they have as a result found in the category of "compassion" depths and nuances they had not seen before. Likewise any Christian who immerses himself or herself now in Buddhism, or in Yoga, may see his or her own tradition, in its weaknesses and its strengths, in a new and creative way;

and perhaps they may be led even to appreciate and embrace it anew! Thus, because there is a "divine covenant" with each form of faith and so genuinely healing truth there, each tradition can encounter another tradition in real dialogue, not only learning from them new truths about the mystery of the divine, but also finding new insight into, criticism of, and even deeper respect for elements of our own tradition. The possibility of real dialogue, therefore, is founded theologically on a strong doctrine of general revelation, a clear sense of the relativity of all that has been characteristic of our own religion and culture as human forms, and a respect and gratitude for the elements of genuine revelation that can come to us out of the "covenant" that God has made with them—as well as the one which we trust forms our standpoint.

Now we reach the second and final question our contemporary situation forces on us. Granted there is a central point—for us the Christ—on which our certainty of and hope for salvation rest, can there be salvation for others who do not share that point or center, whose standpoint is strikingly different from ours? Does or can the Christ bring salvation as well as news of it to those who are *not* his own? This is, let us note, a different though surely related issue from that of the universality of religious truth. There are those who recognize a general revelation, even a natural theology, but affirm salvation only "in Christ" in the sense of explicit faith in Christ or membership in his body. On the other side, there is the sainted Barth, believing in an absolute and unique revelation in Jesus Christ and yet affirming (at least so I read him) that in Christ, the elect one, all men and women are saved. On the other hand, one very creative theme in modern theology has emphasized that these two, the knowledge of God and salvation, are deeply united. Revelation is God's communication of himself, and thus does it involve an "existential knowledge" of God, "acknowledgment" as Barth calls it, that is to say, precisely a saving relation to God. From this point of view, any genuinely received revelation clearly effects as well the beginnings of salvation whenever it appears. I believe this to be true, but much more must be said before our question about universal salvation is answered.

There have been three major grounds for the traditional denial (except in special cases) of salvation to those "outside of faith in Christ or membership in His body," that is, a denial to faithful adherents of other religious traditions. The first is the clear scriptural command against idolatry, the resulting condemnation of "paganism" in both Scriptures, and the assumed restriction of salvation to the adherents of a monotheistic faith. Secondly, there is the conviction that since Jesus, by his death and resurrection, has *effected* as well as revealed salvation, and because he frequently declares himself to be *the* way to it, only those explicitly related or united to him as believers and followers can hope for it. And, thirdly, there is the apparent requirement of explicit faith, including confession of his name, or of explicit Christian works, if salvation is to be possible. We should note that contrary to our common assumptions, "works" do not provide a much wider gate than does "faith," if works be scrupulously defined. In fact, the *point* of the Reformation was that no one at all could get in through the gate of works!

Of course, there have been even in orthodoxy the contrasting themes of the mystery and the unrestrictability of the divine predestination and the divine grace, emphasized by the Augustinian, the Thomistic, and the Calvinist traditions, and expressed in the Catholic insistence on the universality of the divine salvific will. Whenever they appear powerfully, these themes render the above three points at least ambiguous. Salvation, this tradition seems to say, is known and promised here; but since wherever it is, it is God's gratuitous act, it can well be elsewhere, too. Nevertheless, it is fair to say that it was assumed by traditional Catholics and Protestants alike that non-Christians were "lost," bereft of hope of salvation unless they explicitly embraced Christianity. As one eighteenth-century Jesuit missionary to Japan, surveying a population totally without the benefits of the sacrament of marriage, remarked, "It is doleful to contemplate fifty million people living in sin!" If in Christ there is "universal salvation," that merely seems to mean that in him there is all the salvation there is!

Here clearly an even more fundamental redefinition is called for if "universal salvation in Christ" is to include and not exclude adherents of other faiths—as I took it we agree it must. If we ask ourselves why we do in fact think it "must," I suspect we shall be helped to begin that redefinition. On the assumption that we reject the older view principally for theological reasons, let us look for the likely theological grounds for that rejection. I shall briefly mention four.

(1) First is the fact that Christ, however we may understand that reality, is seen by most of us to *manifest* rather than to *effect,* cause, or even to "free" the loving and saving will of God. He represents and embodies, decisively and uniquely, that will; and even his suffering and

death represent and embody rather than effect the participation of God in suffering with us and so the divine rescue of us from it. God's love and will to salvation are here disclosed and promised, and known and acknowledged through Christ's life, death, and resurrection. Since, therefore, the Cross manifests quintessentially the width and depth of the divine love, it cannot itself function to restrict that love; rather it is the revelation of the divine loving will to all creatures. To confine, therefore, the effects of Christ to one community seems to be a misunderstanding of his role as *manifesting* rather than *creating* the freedom of the divine grace.

(2) What is revealed here as the character of the divine saving will is the divine agape. This is a redemptive love whose essence (like the faithfulness of Yahweh) is that it recognizes no barriers to its coming, its presence, or to its effective working. At first, in relation to this love there is neither male nor female, Jew nor Greek, bond nor free, Pharisee nor publican. Subsequently, as Paul and Augustine—and Peter—found, not even the barrier of sin could prevent its coming; and finally—as Luther found—even the barrier of our *continuing* sins was unable to keep that divine "favor" from initiating and effecting salvation. After all these massive barriers have been surmounted, to erect another on the basis of the relativities of culture and of explicit religious traditions—and these have become for us relative in a new way—seems again to be a misunderstanding, in fact a trivialization, of the seriousness and depth of the divine agape.

(3) The same uneasiness about the absolute requirement of explicit faith or explicit works unsettles us when we hear that only confessing Christians are to be saved. Is Mahatma Gandhi then to be excluded and *we* to be let in? The issue of justice aside, this new uneasiness is partly the result of a renewed appreciation of inwardness in religion: to *say* you accept Jesus may not be so important as the hidden commitment of your heart, and a not easily definable quality of love. (That incidentally can appear in very unexpected places!) Also effective, as indicated, is a much deeper sense of the inadequacy of any particular form of faith, including our own, a judgment of inadequacy with which, we are sure, God thoroughly agrees! But most important is a renewed sense of the ambiguity as much of our commitments as of our works. If we depend on the solidity or the perfection of either one, where are we? It is, we know, grace alone, neither the quality of our faith nor of our works, that can bring us salvation. That, we say, is the deepest meaning of Christ as

revelatory of the divine love. But then, having felt freed ourselves from the felt burden of the requirement of perfection with regard to our faith or our works, how can we then say that the same God—or the same Christ—looks with righteous anger on the "un-Christian" character of the faith and the works of the Buddhist? Does the depth of *their* sin, defiance, and idolatry (and note how each of these words are differently defined now!) so contrast with ours as to justify this ultimate division? If the grace of God can overcome my unfaith, idolatry, and lack of love, why not theirs, too? The priority of grace, as Barth sensed, thus moves inexorably in the direction of a love inclusive of all persons and of all relative forms of religion—and so to a concept of a universal salvation in Christ.

Are we then saying that our response of faith and of works is in no way involved in our salvation? God's grace, which we know and of which we are certain in Christ, works in many ways, as does his truth. In each case—so we believe—God elicits our response, some in this form and some in that. And, as we all know well, it is only God—not we—that can assess the reality and the depth of that response. Perhaps the most profound lesson of the symbol of the Last Judgment is not that non-Christians are there condemned, but that it is God and not we who finally looks into the hearts of each and determines the mode of our relationship to God and to one another, and so the final extent of salvation—and from all indications that extent is wider than we can dream.

(4) Finally, the gospel is full—as the contemporary eschatologists have reminded us—of the promise of the final victory of God, of the ultimate sovereignty of God's will, of the redemption of all being. When the "sins" of pagans and of idolators were clear to all of the elect, God's final victory might well have seemed evident enough in their condemnation and in our redemption. But "sin" and idolatry are now much more inward and pervasive realities in our eyes. As we now understand idolatry, none of us, even proper worshippers of the Reformed Faith, are righteous and worthy. Thus, a divine victory, if there is to be one at all, is a *redemptive* rather than a *retributive* victory. This universal hope, as we have sought to make clear, is promised in Christ. But if it is to be a divine *victory,* either for here or for eternity, it must not be confined alone to those who have heard and acknowledge that promise in him.